欢迎：中学汉语课本

HUANYING

An Invitation to Chinese Workbook

JIAYING HOWARD AND LANTING XU

VOLUME 3

3 / 2

PART 2

Cheng & Tsui Company
Boston

Huanying Volume 3 Part 2 Workbook

4th Printing, 2019

25 24 23 22 21 20 19   4 5 6 7 8 9 10

Published by
Cheng & Tsui Company, Inc.
25 West Street
Boston, MA 02111-1213 USA
Fax (617) 426-3669
www.cheng-tsui.com
"Bringing Asia to the World"™

ISBN 978-0-88727-742-9

Illustrations © by Murry R. Thomas, Landong Xu, Qiguang Xu, Lanting Xu, and Augustine Liu

Workbook design by Linda Robertson

Printed in the United States of America

CONTENTS

UNIT 3 青少年时代 **The Teenage Years**

3.1	十点以前必须回家	Must Get Home Before Ten O'Clock	1
3.2	零花钱	Allowances	13
3.3	学开车	Learning to Drive	26
3.4	兼职	A Part-time Job	39
3.5	自由和责任	Freedom and Responsibility	51
3.6	第三单元复习	**Review of Unit 3**	64

UNIT 4 学校生活 **School Life**

4.1	运动会	A Sports Meet	71
4.2	国际文化日	International Culture Day	82
4.3	校外考察	A Field Trip	94
4.4	去南京	Going to Nanjing	107
4.5	家长开放日	Open House Day for Parents	118
4.6	第四单元复习	**Review of Unit 4**	130

ONLINE RESOURCES

Audio Downloads

Throughout this workbook, you will see an audio CD icon  to the left of many exercises. Audio CD icons indicate the presence of audio recordings, which are available as downloadable audio files. For information on how to download the audio files for this workbook, please see page iv of your *Huanying Volume 3* textbook.

TITLES OF RELATED INTEREST

The Way of Chinese Characters, 2nd Edition
The Origins of 670 Essential Words
By Jianhsin Wu, Illustrated by Chen Zheng, Chen Tian
Learn characters through a holistic approach.

Tales and Traditions, 2nd Edition *Volume 1: Fables, Myths, and Historical Figures*
Compiled by Yun Xiao, et al.
Read level-appropriate excerpts and adaptations from the Chinese folk and literary canon.

Cheng & Tsui Chinese Measure Word Dictionary
A Chinese-English / English-Chinese Usage Guide
Compiled by Jiqing Fang, Michael Connelly
Speak and write polished Chinese using this must-have reference.

Visit **www.cheng-tsui.com** to view samples, place orders, and browse other language-learning materials.

第三单元　青少年时代

UNIT 3　The Teenage Years

 3.1　十点以前必须回家
Must Get Home Before Ten O'Clock

一 · 听力练习

 I. Match Them!

Match the phrases you hear in Audio Clip 3-1-1 with the characters in Column B. Enter the corresponding numbers in Column A.

Column A 你听到的	Column B 意思
	过生日
	逛商店
	夜总会
	有考试
	没问题
	准备好
	青少年
	找麻烦
	最流行
	进不去

II. Listen to the recording of Dialogue 1 from Lesson 3.1 first, and then answer the True/False questions in Audio Clip 3-1-2.

	1	2	3	4
对				
错				

 III. Listen to the recording of Dialogue 2 from Lesson 3.1 first, and then answer the True/False questions in Audio Clip 3-1-3.

	1	2	3	4
对				
错				

IV. Listen carefully to the questions in Audio Clip 3-1-4 and answer them according to your own situation. Record your answers on an audio recorder. You have 30 seconds to record your answers. If you do not have a recording device, you can write down your answers below in pinyin or characters.

1. _____

2. _____

3. _____

4. _____

5. _____

6. _____

V. **Rejoinders: In Audio Clip 3-1-5 you will hear five partial conversations, followed by four possible choices designated (A), (B), (C), and (D). Circle the choice that continues or completes the conversation in a logical and culturally appropriate manner.**

Note: Both the questions and the choices will be read only once.

1	2	3	4	5
(A)	(A)	(A)	(A)	(A)
(B)	(B)	(B)	(B)	(B)
(C)	(C)	(C)	(C)	(C)
(D)	(D)	(D)	(D)	(D)

 VI. **Each statement in Audio Clip 3-1-6 describes a Chinese term that is introduced in the "Extend Your Knowledge" section of Lesson 3.1 in your textbook. Listen to the descriptions carefully and write down the term in the space provided. You can take notes while listening.**

Model:

You will hear	You will write
这个词的意思是到达的时间比应该来的时间晚。	迟到

Definition/Description Notes	Name of Term
1.	
2.	
3.	

4.	
5.	
6.	
7.	
8.	

二·综合语言练习

I. **How do you say it in Chinese?**

1.   We are so ready for the Chinese test that there is no chance of an error.

_____

2.   If we leave for the cinema right now, we will still reach it on time.

_____

3.   He always says it will be fine if his test scores are nearly right (pretty close).

_____

4.   The math contest was organized by our school.

_____

5.   In our family, my mother doesn't pay much attention to democracy. All family matters are decided by her.

_____

6. If the sign says teenagers can't enter the nightclub, you shouldn't go in.

_____

7. Because he is a teenager, he still has to listen to his father.

_____

8. My parents have always wanted me to become a white-collar worker in a large company.

_____

9. The electronics store is popular because it sells many fashionable electronic products.

_____

10. If we take the subway, we still have time to arrive home before 10 o'clock.

_____

II. Comprehension Questions

Based on Dialogue 1 from Lesson 3.1, answer the following comprehension questions. Please write your answers in characters in the spaces provided below.

1. 汤姆和朋友为什么要去"红房子"餐厅?

_____

2. 妈妈为什么让汤姆吃完饭就回来?

_____

3. 每次考试前,汤姆都说他准备得怎么样了?

_____

4. 妈妈批评汤姆考试很少得100分。汤姆怎么回答?

_____

5. 妈妈为什么要汤姆十点以前回来?

_____

6. 汤姆为什么觉得十点以前回不来?

_____

7. 汤姆为什么说妈妈不讲民主？

_____

8. 妈妈说什么时候汤姆的事可以由他自己决定？

_____

III.   Pair Activity: What's your opinion?

Step 1: Pick your favorite sentence from the list below. Take turns telling your partner why you like the opinion expressed.

1. 做什么事情都应该努力做到十全十美。
2. 想准备到万无一失的人都会失望 (shīwàng, disappointed) 的。
3. 因为要做到十全十美很难，八九不离十就可以了。
4. 如果每个人都想把事情做到八九不离十，我们的生活里就会有许多问题。
5. 在家里，孩子的事不能都由父母决定。
6. 在学校，学生的事不能都由老师决定。

Step 2: Listen to your partner carefully when s/he speaks and jot down the main points that support his or her position in the left column. After both of you have spoken, write a few "rebuttal" points in the right column. Present the "rebuttal" points to your partner.

话题：	
我同学觉得：	反证 (rebuttal)

IV. True or False

Based on Dialogue 2 from Lesson 3.1, decide if the following statements are true or false.

	对	错
1.吃完饭以后，马克建议大家去夜总会跳舞。		
2.那个夜总会是年轻人喜欢去的地方。		
3.除了大学生、公司白领以外，一些中小学生也去那个夜总会。		
4.十八岁以下的高中生不可以进那个夜总会。		
5.大家没有去看电影，因为好几个同学都要在十点以前回去。		
6.王大明一吃完饭就去找辅导老师。		
7.王大明的家离地铁站不远。		
8.大家去逛一个电子产品店，因为那里的东西很便宜。		
9.因为学校的大门十点关门，所以大家都急着回学校。		
10.学校的看门师傅什么时候都很喜欢找麻烦。		

V. Group Activity: Let's Work Together

Form a small group of three or four people. Your group is going to work on a Chinese history group project. You have a list of tasks that must be done before giving the presentation in class. Discuss the tasks with your group members and decide who will be responsible for each task. Note that when volunteering to do a task, you also need to cite a reason. In order to divide the workload fairly among all members, select one person as the group facilitator (组长). Complete the discussion following the model below.

Model:　组长：请大家看看，中国历史书由谁去借？

　　　　回答：由我去借吧。反正今天我要去图书馆。

组长：请把大家讨论的结果写在下面的表里。

要做的：	由谁做？
1. 借中国历史书	
2. 找关于中国历史的网站	
3. 做中国历史年表	
4. 下载中国画	
5. 下载中国传统音乐	
6. 找一张中国地图	
7. 拍一些/找一些现代中国的照片	
8. 写演讲的报告	
9. 做演讲的幻灯片 (huàndēngpiàn, slideshow)	

VI. **Mixer Activity: How can the teachers improve their teaching?**

Step 1: Write down three things about your classes that you feel can be improved, following the model below and using "老."

Model: 我们的历史课老给学生考试。希望课堂讨论能多一些。

我的建议
1.
2.
3.

Step 2: Based on what you have written, try to find someone who has the same suggestions as you do. Circulate around the classroom and ask your classmates what their suggestions are. You can only ask each student one question. If someone has the same suggestion as you, write down his or her name in the table below. If someone has a different suggestion, write down the suggestion in the box next to "别的建议."

Model:

问题：你觉得老师们怎么样可以把课教得更好?

回答：我觉得汉语课老考试。希望汉语老师多给我们看中国电影和吃中国饭。

我的建议	跟我的建议一样的同学
第一个建议	
第二个建议	
第三个建议	
别的建议:	

Step 3: Report the results of your survey to the class.

VII. Group Activity: Saturday

Suppose a delegation of Chinese high school principals is planning to visit your school this Friday. They are going to spend most of Saturday here before flying to another city at 3:20 p.m. The visitors would like to see as many places as possible while they are here. Your task is to come up with an activity planner.

Step 1: Form a group of three or four. As a group, come up with a list of fun activities for the visitors. You can use the following planner. Make sure that the visitors will have enough time for all the activities.

活动	需要的时间	来得及吗?

Step 2: Take turns presenting your group's activity planner. The group which uses the time most effectively wins.

VIII. You've got mail!

Your pen pal in China has written to you.

Send	Reply	Reply All	Forward	Print	Delete

朋友：你好!

　　昨天我们有英语考试，那个考试挺难的。老师让我们听写20个句子。她说如果我们写错一句可以得B，写错两句得C，写错三句以上就是F。结果，我写错了两句，也没有都写错，就是错了几个词，这个老师就给我C。我觉得她应该去上上数学课，她不会做数学题! 一个考试有20个句子，怎么可以写错几个词就让我得C呢? 你们在美国考汉语，没有这么难吧?

　　为了这个英语考试，上个星期六父母不让我出去玩儿，还请了一个家教来帮我准备考试。那个家教是上海外国语大学的学生。虽然他是第一次来辅导我，可是我马上就喜欢他了。他的英文非常好，而且说话酷极了，我挺喜欢跟他说话的。因为不想让父母知道我们在说什么，我们就用英语聊天。我跟他聊了两个小时的流行音乐、最新的电影、年轻人爱去玩儿的地方、好吃的饭店什么的。时间过得很快，聊完天以后，我们就来不及看书了。我告诉父母，我的英语口语考试已经准备得万无一失了。他们听了很高兴，说我的口语越来越好了，就听见我两个小时老说英语，没听见我说一句中文。

　　可是，我英语考试得了C以后，父母就不再让那个家教来了。他们为我找了一个周末英语学校，要我每个星期六上午去上三个小时的英语课。我跟父母说了半天，考试考得不好不是家教的问题，也不是我的问题，是英语老师不会做数学题。可是他们不听我的。我真的不想去上那个周末英语学校，希望那个家教还能来。你有什么建议吗？快告诉我，好吗？谢谢！

高小文

Use **your own words** to answer the following questions:

1. 为什么高小文抱怨他的英语老师？

_____

_____

2. 为什么高小文喜欢他的英文家教？

_____

_____

3. 为什么高小文的父母要他上周末英语学校？

_____

_____

4. 你觉得高小文的父母的决定对不对？为什么？

_____

汉语课：＿＿＿＿＿＿＿＿＿＿   学生姓名：＿＿＿＿＿＿＿＿＿

日期：　＿＿＿＿＿＿＿＿＿＿

三·写作练习

Write a 100-character email to your pen pal Gao Xiaowen (please refer to Activity VIII above). Give him some suggestions on how to persuade his parents.

Send	Reply	Reply All	Forward	Print	Delete

高小文：你好！

3.2 零花钱 Allowances

一·听力练习

I. Match Them!

Match the words you hear in Audio Clip 3-2-1 with the definitions/explanations in Column B. Enter the corresponding numbers in Column A.

Column A 你听到的	Column B 意思
	一个星期的星期六和星期日。
	学生周末或晚上在饭馆、超市或者商店工作几个小时，挣一点儿零花钱。
	这个词的意思是不贵。
	这个词的意思是，这件事只有你一个人知道。
	这个词的意思是把每天花了多少钱，买了什么东西都写在一个本子上。
	这个词的意思是非常重要的、想不到的事情。
	这个词的意思是一个月的最后几天。
	这个词的意思是计划每个月花多少钱，怎么花，什么的。
	如果你觉得一件事很复杂，要做很多工作才可以完成，那么你可以用这个词来形容这件事。
	中国人过春节的时候常常用这个词。它的意思是有很多钱和贵重的东西。

II. Listen to the recording of Dialogue 1 from Lesson 3.2 first, and then answer the True/False questions in Audio Clip 3-2-2.

	1	2	3	4
对				
错				

III. Listen to the recording of Dialogue 2 from Lesson 3.2 first, and then answer the True/False questions in Audio Clip 3-2-3.

	1	2	3	4
对				
错				

IV. Listen carefully to the questions in Audio Clip 3-2-4 and answer them according to your own situation. Record your answers on an audio recorder. You have 30 seconds to record your answers. If you do not have a recording device, you can write down your answers below in pinyin or characters.

1. _____

2. _____

3. _____

4. _____

5. _____

6. _____

V. Audio Clip 3-2-5 includes three short listening passages. Each passage is followed by two true or false questions based on the content. After listening to each passage, decide whether each statement based on the content is true or false. Each passage will be read twice.

Passage 1

a. 杨朱觉得社会服务虽然有用，但是他没有时间做。   T   F

b. 现在"一毛不拔"说的是一个不喜欢为朋友和社会花钱的人。 T   F

Passage 2

a. 要是孩子的考试考得好，中国父母可能会给他们零用钱。   T   F

b. 在国外，很多父母给孩子零用钱的时候有条件。   T   F

Passage 3

a. 中国的学生一般在月初就把零用钱花完了。   T   F

b. 中国学生在家里很少学怎么理财。   T   F

 VI. In Audio Clip 3-2-6 you will hear some Chinese idioms and proverbs that have been previously introduced. After each idiom/proverb, you will be given 20 seconds to record your definition or explanation. Record your answers on an audio recorder. If you do not have a recording device, you can write down your answers below in pinyin or Chinese characters.

Word Bank

欲速则不达	严师出高徒	读万卷书， 行万里路	青出于蓝而 胜于蓝	桃李满天下

Model:

You will hear	You will say
一分钱一分货	这个俗语的意思是你花的钱跟你买的东西的好坏差不多。

Notes	Possible definition
1.	
2.	
3.	
4.	
5.	

二 · 综合语言练习

I. How do you say it in Chinese?

1. You are really something! You finished 20 math questions in an hour!

_____

2. I am not going to see the ballet tonight. Otherwise, I would have spent all my allowance for this month.

_____

3. During an emergency situation, I can use my parents' bank card.

_____

4. You are really something. Where did you learn about money management?

_____

5. Because I write down how much I spend every time I buy things, I never spend recklessly.

_____

6. Under normal circumstances, my parents give me an allowance of 30 dollars.

_____

7. After learning how to keep an account, I know what I spend my money on.

_____

8. It's only the beginning of the month. You only have 5 dollars left?

_____

II. **How much allowance do they have?**

Based on Dialogues 1 and 2 from Lesson 3.2, find out how much monthly allowance those people on the list have.

姓名	每个月的零花钱	还有其他的钱吗？
玛丽娅		
凯丽		
汤姆		
大卫		

III. **Pair Activity: Under what circumstances do these things happen?**

Both of you have a list of things that people and organizations do. Your task is to find out under what circumstances people or organizations do these things.

Step 1: Fill out the form on your own. Decide what circumstances may lead to the consequences in Column B. Write down the circumstances in Column A. You will use these answers for your partner's questions.

Model: 问题：在什么情况下，学校让学生别去上课？

回答：在天气非常不好的情况下，学校让学生别去上课。

A's sheet

在…情况下	做这些事：
在天气非常不好的情况下	学校让学生别去上课。
	你零花钱不够。
	你不用手机。
	人们打电话给警察。
	你走路去学校。

B's sheet

在…情况下	做这些事：
在天气非常不好的情况下	学校让学生别去上课。
	你不能出去玩儿。
	你不能上网聊天。
	人们去医院。
	父母教孩子理财。

Step 2: Take turns asking each other questions. When your partner gives an answer, write it down on your worksheet.

Step 3: Check your answers with your partner. See if you have got them right.

IV. Mixer Activity: What are the consequences?

Step 1: Answer the following questions. Your answer needs to include the possible consequence if you do otherwise. You will use these answers to answer your classmates' questions.

Model: 问题：你应该把作业做完吗？

回答：我应该把作业做完。**要不然，**老师会批评我。

1. 上课的时候，你可以用手机吗？

   _____。

2. 考试的时候，你可以睡觉吗？

   _____。

3. 你每个月可以花很多钱吗？

   _____。

4. 你上中学的时候可以谈恋爱吗？

   _____。

5. 你在没有紧急情况的时候，能用父母的银行卡吗？

   _____。

Step 2: Circulate around the classroom to interview two students. Make a note of their responses.

	同学一	同学二
上课用手机		
考试睡觉		
花很多钱		
中学谈恋爱		
用父母的银行卡		

Step 3: Share your findings with your class and find out what the common disciplines are for these violations.

V.   **Match Them: A Reckless Action Has an Undesirable Consequence**

Match the actions in the left column with the consequences in the right column.

1. 乱逛商店	一. 被人说是小偷
2. 乱说话	二. 找不到东西
3. 乱花钱	三. 下载到电脑病毒
4. 乱做作业	四. 什么东西都没买到
5. 乱买衣服	五. 老师让我再做一遍
6. 乱放东西	六. 让别人很不高兴
7. 乱下载音乐	七. 月底还没到，钱就没了
8. 乱拿别人的东西	八. 衣服都不合适，都不能穿

VI.   **Mini-Dialogue: Be Smart with Your Money**

A	B
You start • Ask B to go to a concert with you. Tell B how special the concert is. • Tell B the cost of the concert ticket. Emphasize that even though it sounds expensive, the singer is very famous. • Ask if B budgets his or her allowance. • Tell B bookkeeping is helpful to know where the money goes. You keep good books. That's how you never spend recklessly. This way, you always have money for something special.	**Your partner starts** • Tell A you are interested. Ask how much the concert ticket will cost. • Tell A you don't have enough money for the concert. Say something about how you already spent your allowance this month. • Tell A you don't budget. Once the money is out, you stop spending. • Tell A you would like to learn more about bookkeeping. Perhaps when there is a concert next time, you will have enough money to go.
Your partner starts • Tell B the allowance is small so you never have enough. Ask if B has enough for spending. • Tell B you don't work. Occasionally, you get some money from your relatives. • Tell B you call your parents. Ask what B does when s/he needs money.	**You start** • Ask if A's allowance is enough. • Tell A you don't have enough. But you work part-time, so you have some extra. Ask if A works. • Tell A s/he is very lucky. Ask what A does if s/he needs money. • Tell A you have a bank card.

VII. Mixer Survey: Monthly Allowance for High School Students

Step 1: How would you ask these questions in Chinese? In the space below, write the survey questions in Chinese.

1. How much allowance does a US high school student usually get?

   _____

2. Should parents give allowance only after a kid has done house chores（家务）or has done well on a test? Why?

   _____

   _____

3. If money is not an issue, how much allowance would you like to get from your parents?

   _____

4. If you were a parent, how much money would you give your kid?

   _____

Step 2: Circle around the classroom and ask your classmates the survey questions. You can only ask each student no more than two questions. You need to gather at least two responses for each question. Record the responses in the table below.

问题一	学生一	
	学生二	
	学生三	
问题二	学生一	
	学生二	
	学生三	
问题三	学生一	
	学生二	
	学生三	

问题四	学生一	
	学生二	
	学生三	

Step 3: Form groups of four. Share your findings with your group.

VIII. What's your opinion?

Task 1. Many have written on the topic of allowance for children. First, read the following opinions and make sure you understand them:

第一个人的意见：

很多孩子不会理财是因为他们没有钱。过生日或者过圣诞节的时候，他们会得到一点零钱，但是父母不是每个星期或者每个月都给他们钱。还有一些父母说，他们从来不给孩子零花钱。如果一个孩子没有钱，怎么学习理财呢？所以我的建议是：父母应该定期 (regularly) 给孩子零花钱。

Summarize using your own words:

这个人觉得，＿＿＿＿＿＿＿＿＿＿＿＿＿＿＿＿＿＿＿＿＿＿＿

＿＿＿＿＿＿＿＿＿＿＿＿＿＿＿＿＿＿＿＿＿＿＿＿＿＿＿＿＿

第二个人的意见：

不少家长认为 (believe)，只有孩子做了家务以后，才能得到零用钱。我觉得这种想法不对。如果一个孩子不需要钱，他就会不做家务。有时候我对儿子说："如果你打扫厕所，我给你两块钱。"可是我儿子说："我不要那两块钱，我也不打扫厕所。"所以我觉得给零用钱和做家务是两件事，不能放在一起。每个孩子都应该做家务，也应该有零用钱。

Summarize using your own words:

这个人觉得，_____

_____

第三个人的意见：

孩子是怎么学习理财的？多数的孩子都是长大以后，工作了，挣钱了，才开始学习理财。现在不但学校没有理财课，电视上没有理财节目，家长也不教孩子。可是，今天的孩子比以前的孩子有更多的钱，也有更多花钱的机会。他们很小就开始有自己花钱的习惯。如果不教他们，他们很可能会有乱花钱的坏习惯。一般的家长都是等孩子有了坏习惯以后，才开始帮助他们。这时候已经太晚了。所以我觉得孩子一拿到零用钱，家长就应该开始教他们理财。

Summarize using your own words:

这个人觉得，_____

_____

第四个人的意见：

我觉得如果一个孩子学习不努力，就不应该给他零花钱。家长应该让孩子知道，一个人不努力就什么都得不到。也许有人觉得我的想法不对，因为每个孩子都需要有一点儿零花钱。难道一个学习不努力的孩子就不花钱了吗？如果家长不给他们钱，他们可能会去做坏事。可是我觉得要是我在一个公司上班，工作不努力，我会得到钱吗？所以孩子应该从小就学会努力。

Summarize using your own words:

这个人觉得，_____

_____

汉语课：_____   学生姓名：_____

日期：_____

三·写作练习

Based on Activity IX, write your opinion on "allowance for children." You can choose one of the following ways to present your opinion.

1. If you have a completely different opinion from the writers above, state your opinion:

我的意见是，

2. If you totally support one writer's opinion, try to elaborate on it.

我同意第_____个人的意见。因为

3. If you disagree with a writer, write a counter-statement. Try to support your opinion with some facts and examples.

我不同意第_____个人的意见，因为

3.3 学开车
Learning to Drive

一·听力练习

 I. Match Them!

Match the phrases you hear in Audio Clip 3-3-1 with the characters in Column B. Enter the corresponding numbers in Column A.

Column A 你听到的	Column B 意思
	这个词的意思是去城市外面旅游。
	这是一种汽车，可以开得非常快，还可以参加比赛。
	如果你想开汽车，一定要有这个证件。
	这个词的意思是学习怎么开车的课。
	电车、地铁和公共汽车都是这种东西。
	一般来说，这种人是二十一岁以上的人。
	这是一种想开车的人要参加的考试。考试的时候你要开车。

II. Listen to the recording of Dialogue 1 from Lesson 3.3 first, and then answer the True/False questions in Audio Clip 3-3-2.

	1	2	3	4	5
对					
错					

III. Listen to the recording of Dialogue 2 from Lesson 3.3 first, and then answer the True/False questions in Audio Clip 3-3-3.

	1	2	3	4
对				
错				

 IV. Listen carefully to the questions in Audio Clip 3-3-4 and answer them according to your own situation. Record your answers on an audio recorder. You have 30 seconds to record your answers. If you do not have a recording device, you can write down your answers below in pinyin or characters.

1. _____

2. _____

3. _____

4. _____

5. _____

6. _____

 V. Audio Clip 3-3-5 includes three short listening passages. Each passage is followed by two true or false questions based on the content. After listening to each passage, decide whether each statement based on the content is true or false. Each passage will be read twice.

Passage 1

a. 卢生的太太很漂亮，他还有五个很健康的儿子。　　　　　T　F

b. 卢生旅行的时候住在一家很小的旅店里，因为他不喜欢
  跟别人打交道。　　　　　T　F

Passage 2

a. 美国的初中比中国的少一年，高中比中国多一年。　　　　T　F

b. 如果你想上大学，最好先去上一个中专。　　　　　T　F

<u>Passage 3</u>

a. 中国的学生初中毕业的时候已经在学校上了九年学了。　　　T　　F

b. 电影《一个都不能少》讲的是孩子们画饼充饥的事。　　　T　　F

VI. In Audio Clip 3-3-6 you will hear some Chinese idioms and proverbs that have been previously introduced. After each idiom/proverb, you will be given 20 seconds to record your definition or explanation. Record your answers on an audio recorder. If you do not have a recording device, you can write down your answers below in pinyin or Chinese characters.

Word Bank

爱财如命	大手大脚	梦幻泡影
一枕黄粱	挥金如土	画饼充饥

Model:

You will hear	You will say:
望子成龙	这个成语的意思是父母都希望子女很成功。

Notes	Possible definition:
1.	
2.	
3.	
4.	
5.	
6.	

二·综合语言练习

I. How do you say it in Chinese?

1. I am not going on the tour because I don't have time, neither do I have enough money.

_____

2. If the public transportation is convenient, it doesn't matter whether you have a car or not.

_____

3. In a large city, traffic is jammed and parking is not easy.

_____

4. Driving brings you a feeling of freedom.

_____

5. You can take a driver's education course in high school.

_____

6. After taking the driver's education and driver's training classes, you can go for a road test.

_____

7. Only those who have reached 18 years of age can get an official driver's license.

_____

8. In China, most driving schools only admit adults.

_____

9. Teenagers under 18 years old can get a temporary driver's license.

_____

10. Stop dreaming. We don't have a car. Let's take the bus.

_____

II. Pair Activity: Driving vs. Taking Public Transportation

Step 1: Individual work: Study the following list of the pros and cons of owning a car and check off the items that state your opinion on the issue.

开车的好处		公共交通的好处	
开车比公共交通快。		公共交通比开车便宜。	
开车比公共交通方便。		在城里，开车没有公共交通方便。	
开车给人自由。		修车不方便。	
有时候开车比公共交通便宜。比如，出去郊游开车比较便宜。		车太多对环境不好。	
想在哪儿停车就在哪儿停车。有时候要看一看风景或者去洗手间，公共交通不可以在那些地方停车。		在城里，交通太堵，开车开不快。可是坐公共交通，特别是坐地铁会很快。	
要去什么地方，近的远的都很方便。		城里自行车太多，开车不安全。	
开车比坐公共汽车快多了，因为公共汽车每一站都要停下来，让乘客上下车。		在城里，停车不方便。坐公共交通没有停车的问题。	

Step 2: Based on your answers in Step 1, write a short essay on driving vs. using public transportation. Make sure to support your argument with some evidence, using 比如…

_____

_____

_____

_____

_____

_____

_____

_____

_____

Step 3: Get together with your partner and ask each other questions following the model. Make a note of your partner's answers, and then tell your partner's opinions to the class.

Model:　问题：你觉得开车好还是坐公共交通好？

回答：我觉得开车比较自由，因为想去哪儿就可以去哪儿…

III. Did they get it right?

On a website, you saw a discussion of how to get a driver's license in the United States. Based on Dialogue 2 from Lesson 3.3, decide whether the answers are correct.

飞车	12:34 January 20

刚来美国，买了一辆车，很想早日拿到美国驾照。谁知道能很快拿到驾照吗？

世界人	17:20 January 21

会开车吗？会开车就可以拿到驾照了。

飞车	18:15 January 21

十六岁可以拿正式驾照了吗？

世界人	19:13 January 21

可以。你在上高中吧？可以去你们学校上驾驶者教育课和驾驶者培训课。

飞车	20:20 January 21

朋友在教我开车。学会开车以后，我就可以开车了吧？

丽人95	08:11 January 22

不行，要先参加路考。通过路考以后，才可以开车。

飞车	12:20 January 22

怎么才能参加路考呢？

世界人	15:16 January 22

那还不容易？上网定个时间就可以了。

飞车	16:34 January 22

谢谢二位！

Are the instructions correct? Put the correct and incorrect answers into the table below.

对	不对

IV. Pair Activity: Does it matter…?

Your class has organized a "Chinese Culture Night." Because of unexpected events, some of the planned activities need to be changed. The organization committee would like to know how students feel about the changes. Take turns telling each other about the changes. Respond according to how strongly you feel about the changes and write down your responses in the space provided.

Model:

Option 1	Option 2
A: 电影要七点半才开始。你觉得怎么样？ B: 七点还是七点半开始都没有关系 (you don't have a strong opinion) 。你说呢？ A: 我也觉得没有关系。	A: 电影要七点半才开始。你觉得怎么样？ B: 我觉得太晚了 (you have a strong opinion) 。你说呢？ A: 我也觉得太晚了。

原来的计划	现在的计划	你	你同学
电影七点开始	电影七点半开始		
看《美丽上海》	看《长江七号》		
六点晚会开始	六点半晚会开始		
有音乐表演	没有音乐表演		
在大教室举行"中国文化晚会"	在礼堂举行"中国文化晚会"		
晚会有中国小吃	晚会没有中国小吃		
晚会没有中国晚饭	晚会有中国晚饭		
有一个30分钟的武术讲座	有一个15分钟的武术讲座		

V. **Word Game: Name that Word**

Form a group of four. Select one person as the game show host and the other three as contestants. The host will randomly read out the meaning of words from the list below. The contestants will try to name that word. The one who names the word first and correctly will get 10 points. At the end of the game, the host tallies the points and announces the winner.

Note: The words used in this game include some introduced in the "Extend Your Knowledge" section of Lesson 3.3.

Model: 问题：十二岁到十七岁

  回答：青少年

	学生一	学生二	学生三
1. 教别人开车的学校			
2. 十八岁以上的人			
3. 路上有太多的车			
4. 考一个人会不会开车			
5. 去城外旅游			
6. 只有有了这个证件，才可以开车			
7. 这个驾照最多只可以用两年，不能一直用			
8. 开车的人			
9. 教人开车的课			
10. 开着车从一条车道换到另一条车道			
11. 在路口的灯。这种灯有红色的、绿色的和黄色的。			
12. 你觉得前面的车开得太慢，所以你就把车开得快一点，开到那辆车的前边去。			
13. 如果你开车的方向不对，你得拐一个弯往回开。			
14. 马路的旁边			
15. 把汽车往后开，不往前开。			

VI. **Group Activity: Who has the best story?**

Form a group of three or four students. Each group is going to work on a story with the provided sketch. As a group, you need to think of some appropriate and interesting examples for the story. After you have finished the story, share it in class. The class can vote for the best story.

林小平今年16岁，他在达拉斯 (Dallas) 上高中。小平从小就非常喜欢车，特别是看到新车，他就会拍很多照片，还把这些照片发给很多认识和不认识的人。比如，

小平已经上完了驾驶者教育课和驾驶者培训课。他觉得培训课比教育课有意思，因为上培训课的时候，他可以学开车。小平觉得，开车的时候，常常会遇到 (yùdào, encounter) 一些没想到的问题。比如，

　　小平上个星期通过了路考，他急着要拿临时驾照，可是他妈妈不让他现在就拿，要他再等一年，到了十七岁再拿。小平听了很不高兴。可是他妈妈说，小平现在就开车，她会不放心，因为小平还不够负责。比如，

VII. Role Play

Situation 1	
A: You are a new immigrant to the United States and don't know how to get a driver's license. You would like to know the specific steps.	B: You are a high school student in the US. A fellow student who has just immigrated to the United States would like to know how to get a driver's license. Try to be as helpful as you can.

Situation 2	
A: You are living in a large city and your old friend has recently moved here as well. Your friend would like very much to buy a car. You know the problems of owning a car in the city (traffic jams, hard-to-find parking, car theft, traffic accidents, high expenses…) Try to persuade your friend not to buy a car.	B: You just moved to a large city and plan to buy a car. Your old friend advises you not to buy one. Try to let your friend see your point. You need a car to visit all the interesting places in and around the city. Besides, it will be more convenient for you to go to work, shops, sport events, etc. Tell your friend why you need a car.

汉语课：＿＿＿＿＿＿＿＿＿＿＿　　　学生姓名：＿＿＿＿＿＿＿＿＿＿＿

日期：　＿＿＿＿＿＿＿＿＿＿＿

三·写作练习

Your pen pal in China has written to you, asking a few questions about how to get a driver's license in the U.S. After reading your pen pal's letter, write a response to him/her.

Send	Reply	Reply All	Forward	Print	Delete

朋友：你好！

　　因为最近常常考试，所以好久没有给你写信了。希望你一切都好。

　　我们班的学生最近在讨论高中生是不是可以开车的问题。在中国，只有十八岁以上的人才可以开车，这对高中生和对有汽车的学生父母来说都很不方便。因为一是高中生想跟朋友们出去郊游什么的都得坐公共汽车，又贵又麻烦；二是有车的父母每天要接送自己的孩子上学，本来就很堵的马路现在更是车山车海。

　　我听说在美国十六岁就可以开车，是吗？如果你们在美国想考驾照，一般要做什么？希望你来信给我介绍介绍。谢谢！

高小文

Write your response in the email window below (at least 200 characters):

Send	Reply	Reply All	Forward	Print	Delete

3.4 兼职
A Part-time Job

一·听力练习

 I. Match Them!

Match the phrases you hear in Audio Clip 3-4-1 with the characters in Column B. Enter the corresponding numbers in Column A.

Column A 你听到的	Column B 意思
	这个词的意思是去别人家里面为孩子补习功课。
	这是城市里的一个小的地方，有很多家庭、邻居住在这里。
	这是一种可以帮你挣一些零花钱的工作。
	如果你的工作是把一种语言的文章写成另外一种语言的，用这个词很合适。
	这种工作不需要做很多年，常常是有事情做的时候，公司就找一些人去做，做完了以后，这些人就离开这个公司。
	这个词的意思是从早上到晚上。
	这个词的意思是，一个人一说话就让人知道她不是这个国家的人。
	这个词的意思是还可以，不怎么好，也不怎么坏。

II. Listen to the recording of Dialogue 1 from Lesson 3.4 first, and then answer the True/False questions in Audio Clip 3-4-2.

	1	2	3	4	5
对					
错					

 III. Listen to the recording of Dialogue 2 from Lesson 3.4 first, and then answer the True/False questions in Audio Clip 3-4-3.

	1	2	3	4
对				
错				

 IV. Telephone Interview

Mr. Zhang, the manager of an online music store, is giving you a telephone interview about your application for a part-time sales position at his company. Listen carefully to the questions (Audio Clip 3-4-4) and record your answers on an audio recorder. You have 30 seconds to record your answers. If you do not have a recording device, you can write down your answers below in pinyin or characters.

1. _____

2. _____

3. _____

4. _____

5. _____

6. _____

V. Rejoinders: In Audio Clip 3-4-5 you will hear five partial conversations, followed by four possible choices designated (A), (B), (C), and (D). Circle the choice that continues or completes the conversation in a logical and culturally appropriate manner.

Note: Both the questions and the choices will be read only once.

1	2	3	4	5
(A)	(A)	(A)	(A)	(A)
(B)	(B)	(B)	(B)	(B)
(C)	(C)	(C)	(C)	(C)
(D)	(D)	(D)	(D)	(D)

 VI. In Audio Clip 3-4-6 you will hear some Chinese idioms and proverbs that have been previously introduced. After each idiom/proverb, you will be given 20 seconds to record your definition or explanation. Record your answers on an audio recorder. If you do not have a recording device, you can write down your answers below in pinyin or Chinese characters.

Word Bank

马马虎虎	快快乐乐	急急忙忙	灵灵活活
脚踏实地	高高兴兴	安安全全	虎头蛇尾

Model:

You will hear	You will say
望子成龙	这个成语的意思是父母都希望子女很成功。

Notes	Possible definition
1.	
2.	
3.	
4.	
5.	
6.	
7.	
8.	

二·综合语言练习

I. How do you say it in Chinese?

1. After class, he left school in a hurry.

_____

2. He has found a part-time job as an English tutor.

_____

3. His workplace is in the residential area across from the school.

_____

4. A part-time job doesn't require a lot of time. In addition, he can make some money.

_____

5. If there are appropriate opportunities, we'd like to have part-time jobs.

_____

6. This small company can't give me a full-time job.

_____

7. Even though the wage is not high, the work hours are flexible.

_____

8. I get my pay at the end of the month.

_____

9. Working seven to eight hours a week won't affect my study.

_____

10. Even though she has studied English for several years, her listening, speaking, reading and writing are only so-so.

_____

II. What are their job responsibilities?

Based on the two dialogues in Lesson 3.4, write down what jobs David and Maria have and what their job responsibilities are.

大卫的工作：	玛丽娅的工作：
大卫的责任：	玛丽娅的责任

III. Who can reach the finish line first?

Work individually. Match the original plan in the left column with the current situation in the right column by drawing lines between the statements. The student in your class who reaches the finish line first and gets all answers correct wins the game.

1. 他本来要去云南旅游，	A. 后来觉得有车很方便，就买了一辆车。
2. 他本来想去兼职，	B. 可是那个公司现在不需要人。
3. 他本来不想买车，	C. 因为时间不够，不去云南了。
4. 他本来要跟朋友去打网球，	D. 现在会了。
5. 他本来想去那个公司找工作，	E. 可是驾驶学校不收高中生。
6. 他本来要去驾驶学校学开车，	F. 现在知道要当一个好家教不容易。
7. 他本来不会理财，	G. 可是他妈妈说兼职会影响学习，不让他兼职。
8. 他本来觉得当家教很容易，	H. 可是下雨了，他们不能去了。
FINISH	

IV. Mixer Survey: The Best Part-time Job

Step 1: Work in pairs to come up with a list of six most popular part-time jobs that high school students tend to hold. Write the name of these jobs (one example is filled in) in the survey form below.

同意 = 1   不同意 = 0

工作	有意思	工资高	能学新知识	工作时间灵活	总分
1.　在商店卖东西					
2.					
3.					
4.					
5.					
6.					

Step 2: Circulate around the classroom to get your classmates' view on these jobs. If they agree with you, write down 1, if they disagree, write 0. You need to interview at least three students. At the end of your interviews, add the total scores and rank the best part-time jobs in order.

Model:　问题：你觉得在商店卖东西有意思吗/工资高吗/能学到新知识吗…

Step 3: Based on your survey results, write a short essay on a separate sheet of paper with the title: 《最适合高中生的兼职工作》. In your essay, support your argument with statistics from the survey.

《最适合高中生的兼职工作》

_____

_____

_____

_____

_____

_____

_____

_____

_____

_____

_____

V. Should my son have a part-time job?

A Chinese mother has posted a blog entry.

各位网友：

　　东东是我的儿子。上个月他对我说："妈妈，我已经十六岁了。十六岁应该可以去兼职了吧？"我说："你不是在上高中吗？兼什么职啊？还是等高中毕业以后，上了大学再说吧。"

　　我很担心东东的学习。他虽然看书做作业都很快，但是看书是一目十行 (yī mù shí háng, read ten lines at one glance)。看完以后，别人问他书上说了什么，他只知道大意 (main ideas)。作业呢，也是做得马马虎虎，这儿那儿都有错，不是大错，就是小错。有时候我让他看书做作业要认真一点儿。他就说："八九不离十就行了。"可这哪是八九不离十啊，他真的能得到八九十分我就不管他了。现在是每次考试能得七十分就不错了。这样的孩子，怎么还能去兼职呢？他再兼职，就更没时间好好学习了。

　　所以我对东东说，他现在应该一心一意地学习，不应该去兼职。再说，现在找工作也不容易。许多大学毕业生都找不到工作，谁要一个十六岁的高中还没毕业的孩子去兼职呢？我跟东东说了半天，可是他不听我的。这几天，他正在找兼职工作呢。他说要是找到了，不但能赚到一点钱，而且能学到许多在书上学不到的知识。希望大家给我一些建议，我怎么才能说服 (persuade) 东东呢？

Step 1: Based on the blog entry, answer the following questions.

1. 东东为什么要去兼职？

_____

_____

2. 妈妈为什么觉得东东不应该去兼职？

_____

3. 妈妈觉得东东看书做作业有什么问题？

_____

_____

4. 东东的学习成绩怎么样？

_____

Step 2: Work in pairs. First list the pros and cons of Dongdong taking a part-time job. You can list those which are mentioned in the blog, and add anything you think may support either Dongdong's or his mother's position.

兼职的长处	兼职的短处

Step 3: Divide yourselves into two groups. One supports Dongdong taking a part-time job, and the other discourages Dongdong from taking a part-time job. Have a class debate.

VI. Advertise Yourself!

Create an ad to offer your services as a private tutor. You can choose to tutor students on any middle or high school subjects.

Possible academic subjects:

化学	物理	数学	生物	英语	世界历史
美国历史	法语	汉语	西班牙语	拉丁语	地理

Example:

最好的汉语老师

想在这个暑假继续学习汉语吗?想轻松快乐地说好汉语吗?就请跟着我一起学习汉语吧。请给我打电话吧:
Fanny ， 11770760717。

Fanny 有汉语教学经验,对外汉语专业辅导老师,可辅导汉语初级（口语、正音、听说）,初中等 HSK（听力、语法、综合）,中高级汉语视听说,高级 HSK（听力、口试、作文）,汉语流行语等。

家教广告

汉语课：_____   学生姓名：_____
日期：   _____

三 · 写作练习

Get two students' job ads from your teacher and write an email response to each of the ads (no more than 150 characters for each response).

Send	Reply	Reply All	Forward	Print	Delete

Send	Reply	Reply All	Forward	Print	Delete

3.5 自由和责任
Freedom and Responsibility

一 · 听力练习

 I. Match Them!

Match the words you hear in Audio Clip 3-5-1 with the definitions/explanations in Column B. Enter the corresponding numbers in Column A.

Column A 你听到的	Column B 意思
	这个词的意思是一样东西不用给钱就可以拿走。
	这个词的意思是父母每个月给孩子用的钱。
	这个词是说一个人不开通，总是觉得孩子们不可以做这个，也不可以做那个。
	这个词说的是每年七月初中国的高中毕业生要进大学以前的考试。
	如果你帮助我，我帮助你，那这个词来是最适合的了。
	这个成语的意思是，非常好，没有缺点。
	这个词的意思是告诉一个人他需要做什么事情，这样他就不会把这些事情忘了。
	这个词的意思是如果你在一个公司工作，每个月的月底公司给你的钱。
	这个词的意思是中午吃的饭。
	如果做事不注意安全，或者不负责任，最后就可能会有不好的结果。这个词的意思就是这些不好的结果。

II. Listen to the recording of Dialogue 1 from Lesson 3.5 first, and then answer the True/False questions in Audio Clip 3-5-2.

	1	2	3	4
对				
错				

III. Listen to the recording of Dialogue 2 from Lesson 3.5 first, and then answer the True/False questions in Audio Clip 3-5-3.

	1	2	3	4
对				
错				

IV. Listen carefully to the questions in Audio Clip 2-4-4 and answer them according to your own situation. Record your answers on an audio recorder. If you do not have a recording device, you can write down your answers below in pinyin or characters.

1. _____

2. _____

3. _____

4. _____

5. _____

6. _____

V. In Audio Clip 3-5-5 a student is giving a presentation based on a famous Chinese idiom. After listening to the presentation, decide whether each statement based on the content is true or false. The presentation will be played twice. You can take notes while listening.

Notes:

True or False?

	对	错
1. 这个成语故事讲的是淳于髡 (Chún Yúkūn) 和他的国王 (guówáng, king) 的事。		
2. 淳于髡的责任是帮助国王理财。		
3. 国王觉得淳于髡说的那只大鸟就是自己，因为虽然他住在很漂亮的地方，也很能干，可是他什么也不做。		
4. 国王觉得他象大鸟一样，又聪明又能干，工作也非常努力。		
5. 国王听了淳于髡的话很不好意思，因为他把淳于髡吓了一跳。		
6. 现在，"一鸣惊人"这个成语的意思是，聪明的人都不喜欢说很多话，因为他们怕别人听了吓一跳。		

VI. In Audio Clip 3-5-6 you will hear some Chinese idioms and proverbs that have been previously introduced. After each idiom/proverb, you will be given 20 seconds to record your definition or explanation. Record your answers on an audio recorder. If you do not have a recording device, you can write down your answers below in pinyin or Chinese characters.

Word Bank

不知肉味	火烧眉毛	狗急跳墙	鸡飞蛋打	酒肉朋友

Model:

You will hear	You will say
望女成凤	这个成语的意思是，希望自己的女儿很成功。

	You will hear	You will say
1.		
2.		
3.		
4.		
5.		

二·综合语言练习

I. How do you say it in Chinese?

1. You need to be responsible for everything you do.

_____

2. Dating can bring one much happiness as well as trouble.

_____

3. In order to get more freedom, we have to take on more responsibilities.

_____

4. My parents are extremely conservative. They don't allow me to date in high school.

_____

5. Before doing a thing, you should think about the consequences.

_____

6. There is no free lunch in the world. Freedom is not free.

_____

7. I don't think I can always do a perfect job.

_____

8. What you said startles me. I should remind you that we need you to do a perfect job.

_____

_____

9. We should look at the good side as well as the bad side.

_____

10. I hope to find a job with less responsibility.

_____

II. Pair Activity: Freedom and Responsibility

Step 1: Based on Dialogue 1 from Lesson 3.5, categorize the increased freedom and responsibility for a teenager.

自由	责任

Step 2: Work in pairs. Add three more freedoms and corresponding responsibilities to the list above.

Step 3: Form a group of four and share your lists.

III. Pros and Cons of a Part-time Job

Step 1: Decide if the different aspects of a part-time job given in the table below are mentioned in Dialogue 2 from Lesson 3.5.

兼职	说了	没有说
1. 工作时间很灵活，随便什么时候去上班都可以。		
2. 如果要把工作做到十全十美，压力很大。		
3. 有时候工作责任挺大的。		
4. 有时候工作责任很轻。		
5. 做兼职工作，一般工资不太高。		
6. 挣了钱以后，花钱比较自由。		
7. 如果经理是你邻居的朋友，你的工作会比较容易。		
8. 兼职工作常常不安全。		

Step 2: Do you agree with what Maria and David said in the dialogue? Why or why not? Write your opinions in the space provided below.

_____

_____

_____

_____

_____

IV. Board Game: Speaking of...

After throwing the dice, advance the number of spaces shown on the dice, and then make a comment on the object in the corresponding square by using 拿…来说 (for example: 拿这件衣服来说，你穿了一定很好看). If you cannot come up with a sentence, you lose a turn. The first player to reach the finish square wins the game.

	1	2	3
START			
7	6	5	4
8	9	10	11
14	13	12	
FINISH			

V. Pair Activity: In fact…

Suppose a minor incident took place in the school's dining hall. Since the principal is very tough on students, everyone tried to stay out of it by saying they were not there. The principal has assigned you and your partner to find out the truth. After some investigation, you learned the following people were actually in the dining hall. Now you are comparing notes before making a final report to the principal.

Step 1: Take turns to tell each other what you've found out. When your partner speaks, listen carefully and fill in the missing information.

Model: A: 小文说他在宿舍睡觉。

B: 不对吧？他在餐厅里跟同学聊天。

A's sheet

小平	在图书馆看书	
红红		在餐厅买饭
爱丽	在教室休息	
习友		在餐厅发短信
李全	在打乒乓球	
夏静		在餐厅跟同学讨论作业

B's Sheet

小平		在餐厅吃饭
红红	在电脑房玩电脑	
爱丽		在餐厅玩游戏机
习友	在操场上走路	
李全		在餐厅一边吃饭一边听音乐
夏静	在图书馆做作业	

Step 2: Based on the information you've collected, write a short report for the principal by using 其实。

给校长的报告

1. 小文说他在宿舍睡觉，其实他在餐厅跟同学聊天。

VI. Mixer Survey: Your Opinion about Dating

Step 1: Your teacher will assign you a card. First, study the card assigned to you and see if you know the expressions necessary to complete the task written on your card. You can write down your questions in the space provided.

1	2
Find at least one person who believes that students can start dating as early as they wish.	Find at least one person who believes dating while in high school takes too much time and should be discouraged.
Find at least one person who believes that it is impossible to find true love while in high school.	Find at least one person who believes that going to a movie is a good dating activity.

3	4
Find at least one person who believes that it is better to have coffee together than to go dancing when you are on the first date.	Find at least one person who believes that dating should start after high school.
Find at least one person who believes dating should be a secret from your parents.	Find at least one person who believes giving gifts to a date is a good idea.
5	**6**
Find at least one person who believes that dating in high school is unnecessary if you have a lot of friends.	Find at least one person who believes online dating is not safe.
Find at least one person who believes that dating has a negative impact on one's study.	Find at least one person who believes that you should tell your date everything about yourself.

Step 2: Walk around the classroom and interview as many classmates as you can. Make sure that you speak only in Chinese. When it is your turn to respond to the interview questions, try to elaborate on your answers as much as you can. When you are the interviewer, take notes while your classmates are responding to your questions. Later you will be asked to use your notes to prepare for an oral report on the interview results.

Step 3: Form small groups of three or four and give an oral report on your findings.

VII. Group Debate: 做事一定要十全十美吗？

Some students feel that their school work has to be perfect, otherwise they have not done their best. What is your opinion?

Form a small group of four students and debate on the issue. Two of you will be on the affirmative team and the other two on negative team. After the affirmative team finishes its constructive comments, the negative team should conduct a cross-examination and then allow the affirmative team time for rebuttal.

汉语课：_____   学生姓名：_____

日　期：_____

三·写作练习

Step 1: Write five activities that you strongly believe parents should let their children do. For each activity, give at least three supporting reasons. Write in the left column of the table below.

Model:　家长应该让孩子用手机。因为如果孩子有手机，父母跟他们联系很方便。要是有紧急情况，孩子可以马上打电话给父母。还有，手机是孩子们跟朋友联系的好方法。

Step 2: Based on what you've written, write five possible consequences if the child is irresponsible. Write in the right column of the table below.

Model:　家长应该让孩子用手机，可是孩子有时候可能会用得太多，影响学习。

家长应该	可是

家长应该	可是
家长应该	可是
家长应该	可是
家长应该	可是

3.6 第三单元复习
Review of Unit 3

一. 口头报告

Choose one of the topics from the list below to give an oral presentation in class. Your presentation must meet the following criteria:

1. It must have a beginning, a middle, and an end.
2. It must include as much detail as possible.
3. It must last no longer than two minutes.

After you have chosen the topic, please write an outline for your presentation. You can write the outline on a separate sheet of paper. If your teacher allows, you can also transfer the outline to an index card as a reminder when you give the presentation.

Topic 1. 高中生可以自己决定晚上几点回家吗?

Topic 2. 驾驶的法定 (legal) 年龄应该是多大?

Topic 3. 零花钱是高中生学习理财的第一步

Topic 4. 兼职工作对高中生有好处

Topic 5. 高中生对什么样的责任教育有兴趣?

Topic 6. 高中生每周做多长时间的兼职工作比较合适?

二 · 综合语言练习

I. True or False

Based on the Lesson 3.6 Text, decide whether the following statements are true or false.

	对	错
1. 课文要告诉我们中国中学生的作业太多了。		
2. 因为作业太多,多数的中学生每天只能睡七个小时。		
3. 睡觉太少影响了学生的健康和学习。		

4. 广东有一个学生为了做作业，每天最多只能睡六七个小时。		
5. 有一个学生因为很晚睡觉很早起床，只能在上课的时候睡觉。		
6. 在中学有作业太多的问题，在小学没有这种问题。		
7. 课文说很多中学生因为睡觉太少，所以病了。		
8. 有些家长很担心孩子的健康。		

II. The USB has been found!

The following passage describes how Grandma Zhang has found the lost USB. Based on the Lesson 3.6 Dialogue, fill in the missing information.

有一天，张奶奶看到黄黄去了三楼＿＿＿＿＿＿＿。她想因为黄黄去过很多人家，她应该＿＿＿＿＿＿＿＿＿，黄黄有没有把东西＿＿＿＿＿＿＿＿＿＿＿。张奶奶就一家一家地去问，问到了六楼＿＿＿＿＿＿＿＿。王奶奶说：“我一点儿都不懂电脑，也不懂＿＿＿＿＿＿＿＿。”但是王奶奶把黄黄带来的东西＿＿＿＿＿＿＿＿＿。张奶奶在盒子里看到了＿＿＿＿＿＿＿＿。张奶奶想，黄黄把优盘拿走了，因为＿＿＿＿＿＿＿＿＿＿＿＿＿＿＿＿＿＿＿＿＿。

III. Pair Activity: Board Game

Pair up with a partner. Use the words given on each line to form a sentence. Write down your sentences. The one who reaches FINISH first with all of the sentences correct wins the game.

把	准备	已经	考试	我		了	得	万无一失	▼
I have prepared for the test (to the point where there is) no chance of an error.									▼
									▼
决定	公司	经理	由	都	事	得			▼
Everything in the company is decided by the manager.									▼
									▼
乱	我们	花	不	钱	应该				▼
We shouldn't spend recklessly.									▼
									▼
我	银行卡	一般	在	下	情况	用			▼
Under normal circumstances, I use the bank card.									▼
									▼
驾驶	只	成年人	学校	培训					▼
Driving schools only train adults.									▼
									▼
了	了	他	通过	拿到	驾照	路考			▼
He has passed the road test and obtained a driver's license.									▼
									▼
一名	公司	中文	招	正在	翻译				▼
The company is recruiting a Chinese translator.									▼
									▼
应该	会	不好	事	不	我们	的	做	带来	结果	▼
We shouldn't do things that can bring undesirable (bad) consequences.									▼
									▼
FINISH									

IV. Mixer Survey: What are the biggest challenges of being a teenager?

The following questionnaire has ten statements about the challenges of being a teenager.

Step 1: Choose three statements that you strongly agree with.

1. 青少年不容易找到合适的工作。	
2. 青少年在学校里学习压力很大。	
3. 青少年得不到足够 (zúgòu, sufficient) 的零花钱。	
4. 如果青少年谈恋爱，会有谈恋爱的压力。	
5. 如果青少年不谈恋爱，朋友会觉得他/她有点儿奇怪。	
6. 成年人常常不理解青少年。	
7. 社会上许多人不喜欢青少年。	
8. 青少年没有太多的自由，总是被成年人管。	
9. 青少年上网交朋友可能会不安全。	
10. 青少年的事情不能都由自己决定。	

Step 2: Walk around the classroom and interview as many classmates as you can in the time allowed. Take notes on your classmates' responses.

Step 3: Form a group of four. Tally the responses and prepare to give a consolidated report to the class.

V. Role Play: I'm no longer a kid!

Form a group of three.

Situation 1

A	B	C
You would like to go to a nightclub for some fun. Tell your parents you need some spending money and you will come home around midnight.	You are an open-minded parent. You think your child can stay out late sometimes, if there is a good reason. Going to a nightclub is no big deal, but you definitely want your child to pay attention to safety. The only thing you are concerned about is the way your child spends money. You'd like to remind your child to be more frugal.	You are a traditional parent. You don't think your child should go to a nightclub because it is not safe there. Besides, your child should be home by 9 p.m. You don't mind giving the child some money, but you'd like to see the money spent on more useful things than on some wild "fun."

Situation 2

A	B	C
You are 15 years old and would like to learn how to drive. Ask your parent to teach you how to drive. Try to be as persuasive as possible (emphasizing how you have always been very responsible).	You are 17 years old and have a temporary driver's license. Since you were in a minor traffic accident, your parent doesn't allow you to drive any more. You miss driving very much. Tell your parent you can teach your younger sibling how to drive, emphasizing how you have become very responsible. Also try to tell your parent you should be allowed to drive again.	You are a parent. After one of your children got into a car accident, you don't think it's a good idea to let teenagers drive. You will not allow your children to drive until they are 18.

VI. Reading Comprehension: Sleep deprivation?

　　有人做过研究，发现许多美国的青少年睡得不够。多数的美国高中生要到晚上十一二点才睡觉，可是第二天早上六点半左右他们就必须起床了，因为很多学校要学生在七点半就必须到学校。

　　成年人每天睡六七个小时可能够了，但是对青少年来说，每天只睡六七个小时是不够的。科学家发现，青少年每天需要比成年人多睡一两个小时。长期睡得不够不但会影响青少年的健康，而且会带来一些不好的后果。

　　许多交通事故的发生 (fāshēng, occurrence, happening) 是因为有些驾驶者在开车的时候睡着 (shuìzháo, fall asleep) 了。在这样的交通事故中，差不多有一半的驾驶者是青少年。

　　睡觉太少还让有些青少年对学习没有兴趣。因为他们没有休息好，就容易觉得学习太难。还有的青少年在学校没有精神，上课的时候常常睡觉，结果也影响了他们的学习成绩。

　　有人建议，为了让青少年每天睡八个小时，最好的方法是学校晚一点儿开始上课。如果学校从上午八点半或者九点才开始上课，学生就有时间多睡一个小时了。

Complete the following tasks:

1. Come up with a title for this article.

_____

2. 青少年睡得太少带来了哪些不好的后果？

_____

3. 对这个问题，有人提出 (tíchū, propose) 了什么建议？

_____

4. 对这个问题，你有什么建议？

_____

第四单元　学校生活

UNIT 4　School Life

4.1　运动会
A Sports Meet

一 · 听力练习

 I.　Match Them!

Match the phrases you hear in Audio Clip 4-1-1 with the definitions/explanations in Column B. Enter the corresponding numbers and phrases in Column A.

Column A 你听到的	Column B 意思
	体育比赛里包括的运动
	做运动或者开运动会需要用的东西
	足球、篮球、网球、乒乓球等等的比赛
	体育比赛的时候需要用的地方
	长跑、短跑、跳高、跳远等等的比赛
	运动员休息的地方
	打乒乓球的时候用的桌子
	春天开的运动会
	秋天开的运动会
	夏天开的运动会
	冬天开的运动会
	这个世界运动会每四年夏天开一次，2008年这个运动会是在北京开的。

II. Listen to the recording of Dialogue 1 from Lesson 4.1 first, and then answer the True/False questions in Audio Clip 4-1-2.

	1	2	3	4
对				
错				

III. Listen to the recording of the Lesson 4.1 Text first, and then answer the True/False questions in Audio Clip 4-1-3.

	1	2	3	4
对				
错				

IV. Listen carefully to the questions in Audio Clip 4-1-4 and answer them according to your own situation. Record your answers on an audio recorder. You have 30 seconds to record your answers. If you do not have a recording device, you can write down your answers below in pinyin or characters.

1. _____

2. _____

3. _____

4. _____

5. _____

6. _____

V. Audio Clip 4-1-5 includes three short listening passages. Each passage is followed by two or three true or false questions based on the content. After listening to each passage, decide whether each statement based on the content is true or false. Each passage will be read twice. You can take notes in the space provided.

Passage 1

Notes: _____

_____

_____

   a. 如果你参加长跑比赛，你应该去西门报到。   T   F

   b. 如果你是一名体操运动员，你现在正在休息室里喝水，
      那你可以坐在休息室等着报到开始。   T   F

Passage 2

Notes: _____

_____

_____

   a. 虽然北京大街上的小吃很安全，可是很多外国运动员
      还是喜欢在奥运会的餐厅吃饭。   T   F

   b. 在奥运会的餐厅里，中餐、西餐、日餐，什么都有。   T   F

Passage 3

Notes: _____

_____

_____

   a. 棒球是在美国开始的。   T   F

   b. 历史上第一个棒球比赛的方法是在1839年定的。   T   F

   c. 棒球是在十九世纪 (shìjì, century) 介绍给日本的。   T   F

VI. In Audio Clip 4-1-6 you will hear some Chinese idioms and proverbs that have been previously introduced. After each idiom/proverb, you will be given 20 seconds to record your definition or explanation. Record your answers on an audio recorder. If you do not have a recording device, you can write down your answers below in pinyin or Chinese characters.

Word Bank

百发百中	丢三落四	百步穿杨	健步如飞	争先恐后

Model:

You will hear	You will say
多子多福	这个成语的意思是儿子越多家里的生活就越好。

You will hear	You will say

二·综合语言练习

I. How do you say it in Chinese?

1. Our class will get the sports equipment ready for the school's sports meet.

_____

2. The sports meet has track and gymnastics competitions.

_____

3. All of the ball games will be held in the school's sports field.

_____

4. The sports meet has many competition events and should be very lively.

_____

5. If he had a focal point in his work, he wouldn't have missed this or that.

_____

6. Our class will be divided into four small groups.

_____

7. The coffee shop supplies drinks and snacks all day long.

_____

8. There is enough space to put three tables in the room.

_____

9. In front of my house, there is enough space to park two cars.

_____

10. The restaurant has a seating capacity of 80 (the restaurant has enough space to seat 80 people).

_____

II. Are these our tasks?

Tom doesn't know what tasks his class is supposed to do for the school's sports meet. Based on the Lesson 4.1 Dialogue, answer his questions.

汤姆的问题	需要	不需要
1. 我们班需要准备田径比赛的运动器材吗？		
2. 我们班需要准备比赛场地吗？		
3. 我们班需要负责运动员休息室吗？		
4. 我们班需要供应茶水和点心吗？		
5. 我们班需要把乒乓桌放在教室楼前边吗？		
6. 我们班需要准备球类比赛的运动器材吗？		
7. 我们班需要准备体操比赛的场地吗？		
8. 我们班需要负责大家的午饭吗？		

III. Pair Activity: Which sport events should we go to?

You and your partner truly enjoy each other's company and always do things together. For the school's sports meet, each of you is interested in certain events. Some of your interests are the same and some are different. Based on the Lesson 4.1 Text, try to work out a schedule that will make both of you happy.

A's sheet

我想去看以下的比赛：				
个人田径	男子乒乓球	男子篮球	男子羽毛球	女子体操

B's sheet

我想去看以下的比赛：				
团体田径	男子体操	女子体操	女子排球	男子篮球

我们的计划：

时间	比赛项目	比赛场地

IV. Mixer Bingo: Is there enough room for…?

Step 1: Answer the questions in each square, based on your real or imaginary situation. Write your answers in the bingo grid below.

一辆车里坐得下几个人？ _____	一个电影院里坐得下多少人？ _____	你家前边停得下几辆车？ _____
这个教室放得下多少个桌子？ _____	你的房间放得下几张床？ _____	你的书包放得下几本书？ _____
学校的礼堂坐得下多少人？ _____	你吃得下几个汉堡？ _____	你家住得下几个人？ _____

Step 2: Walk around the classroom and ask your classmates the questions in the bingo grid. You can only ask each student one question. When a student's answer is the same as yours, you can cross out that square. The one who crosses out three squares in a row first—horizontally, vertically, or diagonally—wins the game.

V. Pair Activity: Celebrate Creativity!

Step 1: Work individually. Choose three verbs from the list below. Use the structure "把 + Noun 1 + Verb + 成 + Noun 2" (with the meaning of "transforming a thing from one form into another") to make three phrases.

分成	变成	写成	做成
翻译成	画成	说成	改成

Model: 把小说写成电影

1. _____

2. _____

3. _____

Step 2: Use the phrases you've written to ask your partner whether he or she can do it.

Model: 问题：你能把小说写成电影吗？

　　　　　回答：能。(or 不能。)

VI. Pair Activity: Guess who my favorite athlete is!

Pair up with a partner. Think of one athlete that you like the most, but do not tell your partner. Your partner must ask questions to find out which athlete you have in mind. Remember, your partner can only ask "yes" and "no" questions, and you can only answer "yes" or "no." Once the game is over, switch places. It is time for you to guess your partner's favorite athlete.

Model: 问题：这个运动员打乒乓球吗？

　　　　　回答：对。(or 不。)

　　　　　问题：这个运动员是美国人吗？

　　　　　回答：对 or 不。

　　　　　……

VII. **You've got mail!**

Step 1: Your pen pal in Shanghai has written to you. Find out what's going on in his life.

Send	Reply	Reply All	Forward	Print	Delete

真对不起，上个星期我就收到你的Email了，可是到了今天才给你写信。因为要参加学校运动会的比赛，上个星期我特别忙，每天一下课就去训练，常常训练到天黑才回家。我告诉过你了吗？这学期我不但参加了学校的排球队和游泳队，还参加了田径队。

这次学校的运动会，有球赛、田径比赛和体操比赛，没有游泳比赛。我本来应该参加上午的长跑和跳高比赛，还有下午的排球比赛。第一项比赛是长跑，我得了第三名。大家都为我高兴。长跑完了以后，我去跳高。那天参加跳高比赛的人不太多，我进了前六名。我们班的同学老师都特别高兴，他们说，看上去我跳高也一定能得到好成绩。可是比赛到一半的时候，我把腿摔伤了，结果跳不了了。因为腿摔坏了，下午的排球比赛我也没参加。大家都说非常可惜 (kěxī, it's a pity)。休息了几天以后，我的腿已经不太疼了，走路也没有问题了。

这两个星期你在做什么？写信告诉我，好吗？

你的朋友，

丁小星

Answer the following questions based on the email above.

1. 丁小星为什么没有马上写信？

_____

2. 丁小星本来要参加哪几个比赛？后来参加了哪几个比赛？

_____

_____

3. 丁小星比赛的成绩怎么样？

_____

4. 跳高比赛的时候，出了什么事？

_____

Step 2: Write five questions in Chinese that you would like to know about the sports meet that Ding Xiaoxing attended.

1. _____

2. _____

3. _____

4. _____

5. _____

汉语课：_____   学生姓名：_____

日期：_____

三·写作练习

You will conduct a WebQuest.

Step 1: Conduct an Internet research on the 2008 Summer Olympics in Beijing and see how many questions in Section 2 you can answer. Here are some suggested websites:

http://www.beijing2008.cn/

http://www.beijing2008.cn/venues/

http://images.beijing2008.cn/lib/zyz_peix/courses/01/main.htm

http://www.xinhuanet.com/olympics/totalmedal.htm

http://sports.espn.go.com/oly/summer08/medals

http://news.xinhuanet.com/olympics/2008-08/18/content_9461045.htm

Step 2: Answer the following questions:

1. 下面的运动场馆有哪些的比赛？

运动场馆	比赛项目
国家体育场	
国家体育馆	
国家游泳中心	

北京大学体育馆	
首都体育馆	

2. 一共有多少个比赛项目是在北京的奥运会场馆举行的？

    _____

3. 在国家游泳中心的游泳比赛中，女子五十米自由泳比赛得第一名的
是哪国人，第二名是哪国人？第三名呢？

    _____

    _____

4. 在二零零八年北京奥运会上，哪个国家得的金牌最多？哪个国家得
的银牌最多？哪个国家得的铜牌最多？

    _____

    _____

5. 在得到十块以上奖牌的国家中，哪些国家得的奖牌数一样多？

    _____

Step 3: Create three trivia questions in Chinese about the 2008 Beijing Olympics. You will be sharing these questions with your classmates.

北京奥运知识竞赛问题：

1. _____

回答：

2. _____

回答：

3. _____

回答：

4.2 国际文化日
International Culture Day

一・听力练习

 I. Match Them!

Match the words you hear in Audio Clip 4-2-1 with the definitions/explanations in Column B. Enter the corresponding numbers and words in Column A.

Column A 你听到的	Column B 意思
	中国人炒菜用的烹调器材
	蒸包子用的烹调器材
	烤面包、烤肉用的烹调器材
	喝汤用的餐具 (utensils)
	把肉切成小块用的餐具
	中国人吃饭时候夹菜用的餐具
	吃西餐时夹菜用的餐具
	吃饭擦 (cā, to wipe) 嘴用的纸
	喝水用的餐具
	放炒好的菜用的餐具
	放汤用的餐具

II. Listen to the recording of Dialogue 1 from Lesson 4.2 first, and then answer the True/False questions in Audio Clip 4-2-2.

	1	2	3	4
对				
错				

 III. Maria and her classmates are discussing what they need to prepare for the "Chinese Chef" cooking competition next weekend.

Step 1: Listen carefully to their discussions in Audio Clip 4-2-3 and complete the following two tasks:

(1) Write the number of each item the club needs in preparation for the competition.
(2) Write down the name of the person who is in charge of bringing each item.

需要准备的东西	要多少	由谁负责
盘子		
刀叉		
筷子		
杯子		
餐巾		
蒸笼		
炒菜锅		
烤箱		
菜刀		
砧板		
茶包		
茶壶		

Step 2: Listen again and write down what dishes each group will be demonstrating.

小组长	地方菜	食品名
汤姆		
明英		
大卫		
玛丽娅		

IV. Listen carefully to the questions in Audio Clip 4-2-4 and answer them according to your own situation. Record your answers on an audio recorder. You have 30 seconds to record your answers. If you do not have a recording device, you can write down your answers below in pinyin or characters.

1. _____

2. _____

3. _____

4. _____

5. _____

V. Audio Clip 4-2-5 includes four short listening passages. Each passage is followed by two true or false questions based on the content. After listening to each passage, decide whether each statement based on the content is true or false. Each passage will be read twice.

<u>**Passage 1**</u>

Notes: _____

_____

_____

a. 肉夹馍是西安人吃的三明治。   T   F

b. 汤姆觉得肉夹馍的名字不适合，因为其实是馍夹肉。   T   F

Passage 2

Notes: _____

_____

_____

a. 凯丽负责介绍小笼包的历史。   T   F

b. 凯丽小组的其他人要做四种不同馅儿(xiànr, filling)
的小笼包。   T   F

Passage 3

Notes: _____

_____

_____

a. 今天食堂的菜里，有两个炒菜和一个汤。   T   F

b. 如果你要买二十个饺子和一碗酸辣汤，你只要花
四块五。   T   F

Passage 4

Notes: _____

_____

_____

a. 南甜北咸，东辣西酸，说的是美国各地有不同的
饮食习惯。   T   F

b. 在中国的八大菜系里，只有三个在美国很有名。   T   F

二·综合语言练习

I. **How do you say it in Chinese?**

1. Chinese culture has many aspects. Which aspect are you interested in?

_____

2. There should be some novel ideas in this year's Culture Day activities.

_____

3. Our school takes cultural activities seriously.

_____

4. The geographic environment and the climate affect agricultural produce.

_____

5. Food from different regions is not the same. Each has its own characteristics.

_____

6. The audience will taste the dishes first and then vote for the best one.

_____

7. The cooking show needs a big wok and a steamer.

_____

8. We had a lively discussion but haven't come to a decision.

_____

9. One of the lectures is on the food culture of China.

_____

10. Although the movie may not be considered the very best, it is definitely one of the best.

_____

II. Meeting Notes

When the class had its meeting (see Dialogue 1 from Lesson 4.2), a student took some notes. Compare the notes with the dialogues. Are the notes accurate?

	对	不对
1. 在国际文化日，汉语班要介绍中国文化。		
2. 国际文化日的活动都很有新意。		
3. 汉语班的同学建议国际文化日可以唱歌、跳舞、看电影。		
4. 有人提议可以介绍中国的食文化。		
5. 有人提议介绍中国文化的十个方面。		
6. 汉语班的活动之一是烹调表演。		
7. 除了烹调表演以外，可以介绍中国各地食品的特点。		
8. 汉语班要分成四个小组，每个小组要做四个菜。		
9. 有人提议还应该让大家看中国地理的电影。		
10. 来参加国际文化日的观众可以尝一尝中国菜。		

III. What is needed for the cooking show?

Based on Dialogue 2 from Lesson 4.2, circle the items that are mentioned. If the information is given, also write down the quantity needed.

东西	要多少？	东西	要多少？
		咖啡杯	
小刀子			
大盘子			
		热水瓶	
		微波炉	
冰箱			

IV. Mixer Survey: One of the Best

Suppose a Chinese delegation is coming to visit your town. They would like to know something about your town before arrival.

Step 1: Complete the bingo grid on your own.

_____是最好的中国饭店之一。	_____是最有意思的公园之一。	_____是最好的百货商店之一。
_____是最大的超市之一。	_____是最舒服的旅馆 (hotel) 之一。	_____是最好的书店之一。
_____是最有名的旅游点之一。	_____是最好的美国饭店之一。	_____是最美丽的地方之一。

Step 2: Walk around the classroom and interview your classmates. Speak in Chinese and try to talk to as many classmates as you can in the time provided. You can only ask and answer one question at a time. If someone has the same choice as yours, you can cross that square out. Whoever crosses three squares in a row wins the game.

Model:　问题：哪个是最有名的旅游点之一？

V. Pair Activity: We have Different Opinions

You and your partner are going to have a fun night out. Each of you has decided on three activities that you would like to do. Now you are comparing notes.

Step 1: Write three positive comments about the places you want to go or the things you want to do.

Model:　我打算去博物馆看一看，因为博物馆非常有意思。

A's sheet

你打算	因为
1. 去"天天书店"逛一逛	
2. 去"小意大利"饭店吃晚饭	
3. 去看电影《哈里·波特》	

B's sheet

你打算	因为
1. 去"北京饭店"吃饭	
2. 去溜冰场溜冰	
3. 去"新星"俱乐部跳舞	

Step 2: Take turns telling your partner what you plan to do. Your goal is to agree on three activities that both of you would like to do. Listen to your partner carefully. If you like your partner's idea, write down the activity in the table below. If you disagree, use "算不上" to express your opinion.

Model: 你同学：我打算去博物馆看一看，因为博物馆非常有意思。

你：博物馆算不上有意思。

你们打算
1.
2.
3.

VI. Pair Activity: Make a Master Schedule

You are tasked to prepare a master schedule for your school's "International Culture Day." You already have short announcements from various language classes and student clubs. Consolidate this information into a master schedule.

中国的"食文化" 时间：上午8点–10点 地点：105大教室 汉语班要介绍中国最有名的地方菜。并要举行烹调表演。欢迎大家来尝一尝我们做的中国菜。	拉丁舞表演 下午1点，跳舞俱乐部要在学校大礼堂表演拉丁舞。请大家参加。
日本茶道 (Tea Ceremony) 日语班上午9点到9点半在206教室表演日本茶道。大家可以前来参加。	意大利电影 下午1点到3点在大教室放意大利电影《美丽人生》。意大利俱乐部将供应咖啡和意大利点心。
《一千零一夜》(1001 Nights) 时间：上午10点到11点 地点：211教室 阿拉伯语班要表演话剧《一千零一夜》的故事之一。	法国艺术历史讲座 时间：上午11点 地点：101教室

中国武术表演	美国足球
中国武术俱乐部上午10点将在教室楼前表演中国武术，欢迎大家来观看。	你想知道美国足球是什么样的吗？美国学生俱乐部下午1点到2点在学校操场举行美国足球比赛。
俄国古典芭蕾舞	国际食品
11点到1点，俄语班将在学校大礼堂放电影《天鹅湖》。欢迎大家参加。	时间：11点到12点 地点：学生餐厅 各个外语班和俱乐部准备了各国食品，欢迎大家购买。

时间	地点	活动

VII. Picture Description: 熊猫灵灵的生日会

Write a story about Panda Ling Ling's birthday based on the pictures below. Your story must have a beginning, a middle, and an end, and must use the following structures:

除了……以外，还……　　　　　　……之一

不但……还……　　　　　　　　　要不是……就……了

汉语课：＿＿＿＿＿＿＿＿＿   学生姓名：＿＿＿＿＿＿＿＿＿

日期：　＿＿＿＿＿＿＿＿＿

三·写作练习

Choose one Chinese holiday food (e.g. 饺子、月饼) and write a 100–150 character essay about this food. What is the history of this food? During which festival do the Chinese eat it? What is the cultural significance of this food (symbolic meanings, etc.)?

4.3 校外考察
A Field Trip

一·听力练习

 I. Match Them!

Match the words you hear in Audio Clip 4-3-1 with the definitions/explanations in Column B. Enter the corresponding numbers and words in Column A.

Column A 你听到的	Column B 意思
	在河边、海边停船的地方。
	记账、理财的公司都是这种公司。
	为了不忘记一个人或者一件事造的建筑或者建立的博物馆。
	这个词的意思是为了保护环境，大家种树、种花，让环境是绿色的，不只是灰色的大楼。
	这是一种有很多家庭住的楼房。
	这样的建筑只有一个家庭在里面住。
	这是种菜的地方。
	这是买东西的意思。
	这是一种公司或者社区提供的交通。只有在这个公司工作的和在这个社区住的人才可以坐。
	这个词是用来说住在一个社区里的人。

II. Listen to the recording of Dialogue 1 from Lesson 4.3 first, and then answer the True/False questions in Audio Clip 4-3-2.

	1	2	3	4
对				
错				

 III. Listen to the recording of Dialogue 2 from Lesson 4.3 first, and then answer the True/False questions in Audio Clip 4-3-3.

	1	2	3	4
对				
错				

IV. Listen carefully to the questions in Audio Clip 4-3-4 and answer them according to your own situation. Record your answers on an audio recorder. You have 30 seconds to record your answers. If you do not have a recording device, you can write down your answers below in pinyin or characters.

1. _____

2. _____

3. _____

4. _____

5. _____

6. _____

V. Audio Clip 4-3-5 includes three short listening passages. Each passage is followed by three or four true or false questions based on the content. After listening to each passage, decide whether each statement based on the content is true or false. Each passage will be read twice.

Passage 1

Notes: _____

_____

_____

a. 参观科学城小区的人是说话人的亲戚。   T   F

b. 科学城小区的绿化很好，居民们可以在小区中心的湖
   边走走，休息休息。   T   F

c. 科学城小区里用的电都是太阳能。   T   F

d. 如果你想住在科学城小区，你可以在那儿买一套公寓，
   或者一个别墅。   T   F

Passage 2

Notes: _____

_____

_____

a. 上海的黄浦公园在黄浦江的东边。   T   F

b. 黄浦公园最早有一个英文名字，意思是公共花园。 T   F

c. 黄浦公园这个名字是1946年开始用的。   T   F

Passage 3

Notes: _____

_____

_____

a. 参加中国人的酒席时，一定要先问问服务员再坐下来。　　T　　F

b. 中国人的酒席，一般是先上冷菜，再上热汤，然后是
炒菜，最后是甜点。　　　　　　　　　　　　　　　　T　　F

c. 虽然你很喜欢吃色拉，如果你请中国人吃饭，也不能
只要四种色拉，两个炒菜。因为炒菜一定要比冷菜多。　T　　F

d. 不管你喜欢不喜欢酒席里的菜，你都要说，对不起，
今天没有什么好菜。下次一定请你吃真正的中国菜。　　T　　F

VI. In Audio Clip 4-3-6 you will hear some Chinese idioms and proverbs that have been previously introduced. After each idiom/proverb, you will be given 20 seconds to record your definition or explanation. Record your answers on an audio recorder. If you do not have a recording device, you can write down your answers below in pinyin or Chinese characters.

Word Bank

多姿多彩	远亲不如近邻	百花齐放，百家争鸣	左邻右舍	邻里相助

Model:

You will hear	You will say
多子多福	这个成语的意思是儿子越多家里的生活就越好。

You will hear	You will say

二·综合语言练习

I. How do you say it in Chinese?

1. The students went on a field trip to a memorial museum.

_____

2. Starting in the mid-19th century, the city became one of the financial centers in the world.

_____

3. These large buildings were built in the 1920s.

_____

4. A road was built along the river.

_____

5. The historical buildings are protected by the government.

_____

6. This international community was established in the 1990s.

_____

7. The economy developed quickly, and many new companies were set up.

_____

8. More than 1000 residents from more than 20 countries live in this community.

_____

9. The environment is very good, with a lot of greenbelts, and fresh (good) air (quality).

_____

10. It is very convenient for shopping, transportation, and (getting) services.

_____

II. The History of the Bund

After coming back from the field trip to the Bund, a student wrote a short summary of the history of the Bund. Compare the summary to Dialogue 1 from Lesson 4.3 and write down at least three discrepancies in the space provided below.

上海外滩的历史是这样的：

外滩是1844年开始发展的。那一年，英国人在外滩造了码头和一条叫Bund的大马路。从1848年开始，英国人在外滩开了不少公司。到了二十世纪的二十年代和三十年代，越来越多的公司和银行搬到外滩。这些公司和银行多数是外国的，但是也有一些是中国的。这些公司和银行在外滩造了许多大楼。这些大楼各式各样，现在都是上海政府要保护的历史建筑。现在这些大楼都是政府的办公楼。

对话	学生的总结 (summary)

III. The "East Sea" International Community

Based on Dialogue 2 from Lesson 4.3, find at least three positive features of living in the East Sea International Community. Try to fill in as much detail as possible.

| |
| |
| |
| |

IV. Match Them!

Step 1: Match the events in the left column with the dates in the left column.

美国独立	1. 十五世纪九十年代
哥伦布 (Columbus) 到美洲	2. 第二世纪初
联合国成立 (establish)	3. 二十世纪七十年代
美国人第一次去月亮	4. 十八世纪七十年代
发明因特网	5. 二十世纪四十年代
发明纸	6. 二十世纪六十年代

Step 2: It's your turn! List 3–5 historical events in the left column and test your classmates' knowledge of history. You can even collect all the questions from your classmates and play a history trivia game.

历史事件	世纪和年代

V. Pair Activity: Mini-Dialogue

A: You start	B: Your partner starts
• Tell B your class went on a field trip to a historical building last Wednesday.	• Ask A when the building was built.
• Tell B it was built in the 18th century.	• Ask A if the building is a residence or a commercial building.
• Tell B it is a commercial building. It was used by a bank and now the town government has bought it.	• Ask A about the style of the building.
• Tell B it was in a Victorian (维多利亚, Wéiduōlìyà) style.	• Ask A if anyone can go inside to take a look.
• Tell B it is now a protected historical building. It is open to the public every Wednesday.	• Tell A you would like to visit the building someday.
A: Your partner starts	**B: You start**
• Ask B what's special about this residential community.	• Tell A you visited a new residential community last weekend.
• Ask B who has planned the community.	• Tell A it not only has houses, but also has stores and services.
• Ask B what suggestions the local residents made.	• Tell A it was planned by the city government, but the local residents also made a lot of suggestions.
• Tell B the community sounds very interesting and you would like to visit it someday.	• Tell A the residents want a place where public transportation, shopping, schools, and services are all convenient.

VI. Mixer Survey: Community Improvement Plan

In order to serve young people's needs, which were neglected in the past, the city planning committee would like to get input from younger residents before making a community improvement plan. Your class has been chosen to draft a survey form in Chinese. To draft a good survey form, you will first find out what your classmates would like the community to have.

Step 1: Read the following interview sheet. Add two more questions that you think are important to a good community. Go around the classroom and interview three students using the following questions. Record your findings on the interview sheet.

问题	同学一	同学二	同学三
1. 社区应该有图书馆吗？			
2. 社区应该有青少年活动中心吗？			
3. 社区应该有公园吗？			
4. 社区应该有方便的公共交通吗？			
5. 社区购物应该方便吗？			
6. 社区应该有不同的服务吗？			
7. 社区应该有电影院吗？			
8. 社区应该可以免费上网吗？			
9.			
10.			

Step 2: Form a group of three or four students. Based on your findings, design a list of survey questions (at least 12). The questions should be specific. Make sure to write them so that the survey respondents can simply check 应该 or 不应该。

问题	应该	不应该

VII. Get the Essential Information

The following is an advertisement for a newly developed residential area. After reading the ad, answer the content questions.

小区名称：安桥国际社区
小区地址：绿地大道788号
所在区域：安江
绿化率：40%
开发商：安江发展公司
物业公司：安江房地服务公司
小区介绍： 　　"安桥国际社区"在安江的东南边，离上海市中心50公里，离浦东国际机场75公里。附近有方便的公共交通：公共汽车、轻轨(qīngguǐ, light rail)、火车，一个小时可以直达上海市中心，是"上海的后花园"。安桥国际社区附近有大型超市、大上海国际商业中心、绿地国际购物中心、农业银行、中国银行、工商银行。生活购物交通都非常方便。附近还有：绿地九年制国际学校、安桥幼儿园、安桥小学、安桥中学、安桥医院、安桥公园、绿地国际大酒店、安江影城等。这里将成为安江地区新的金融中心、商业中心、教育中心和文化中心。

1. 安桥国际社区在什么地方？

_____

2. 有哪些公共交通可以到达安桥国际社区？

_____

3. 安桥国际社区附近有哪些学校？

_____

4. 为什么说安桥国际社区将成为金融和商业中心？

_____

VIII. Economic Development in My Area

Task: You are asked to give a presentation on the economic development in your area.

Step 1: Study the additional vocabulary introduced in the "Extend Your Knowledge" section of Lesson 4.3. Then use an outline map of your region to create a poster or a slideshow presentation indicating the types of industries in your region. The sample map below may give you some ideas as you create your own map.

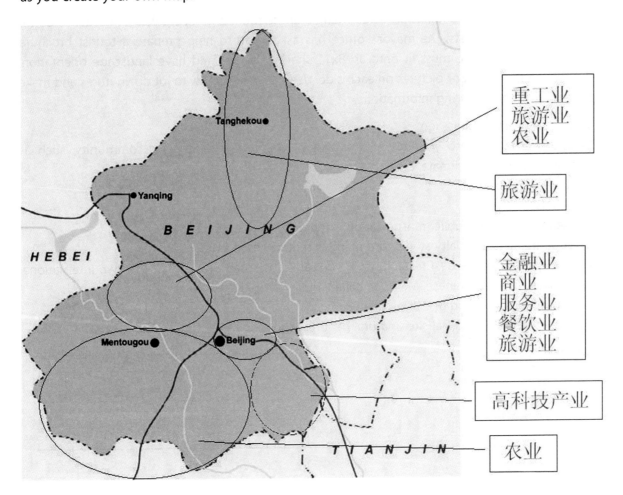

Step 2: Give the presentation orally in your class. Ask your teacher's permission if you need to use a note card during the presentation.

汉语课：_____   学生姓名：_____

日期：_____

三·写作练习

Your town, a hot tourist spot, has attracted many Chinese tourists in recent years. In order to better serve the Chinese tourists, the mayor's office has asked you to help prepare a tourist brochure in Chinese. The brochure must fit onto an 8x11 sheet of paper, and have landscape orientation, with three panels of text or pictures on each side. Use the space below to jot down notes and make sure to include the following information:

1. A general welcome message
2. A brief introduction to your town (the general characteristics of your community, such as location, population, climate, etc.)
3. Local resources:
   a. Hotels
   b. Nearby facilities (public transportation, shopping, services, etc.)
   c. Supermarkets, specialty stores, and markets that sell food products
   d. Three to five of the best restaurants in your area (be sure to include one or two international cuisines, such as Chinese, Mexican, Italian, etc.)
   e. Typical regional food or cuisine (if any)
   f. Other features: historical sites, natural beauty, economic development, etc.

_____

_____

_____

_____

_____

_____

_____

4.4 去南京
Going to Nanjing

一·听力练习

I. Match Them!

Match the words/phrases you hear in Audio Clip 4-4-1 with the definitions/explanations in Column B. Enter the corresponding numbers and words/phrases in Column A.

Column A 你听到的	Column B 意思
	这是一个风景非常美，游客愿意来的地方。
	去晚上的小吃街看看，吃吃饭，买买东西。
	很大的给游客坐的车，但是不是公共交通。
	这个比赛上大家要给听众讲话。
	这是出门旅行的时候带的大包小包。
	这样的箱子可以让你拉着走，比较方便。
	这个词的意思就是环境保护。
	这是用手机发给朋友和家人的电邮。
	也叫墨镜，是有太阳的时候戴的。
	这个词的意思是你每天要用的牙膏、牙刷、什么的。

II. Listen to the recording of the Lesson 4.4 Text first, and then answer the True/False questions in Audio Clip 4-4-2.

	1	2	3	4
对				
错				

III. Listen to the recording of the Lesson 4.4 Dialogue, and then answer the True/False questions in Audio Clip 4-4-3.

	1	2	3
对			
错			

IV. Listen carefully to the questions in Audio Clip 4-4-4 and answer them according to your own situation. Record your answers on an audio recorder. You have 30 seconds to record your answers. If you do not have a recording device, you can write down your answers below in pinyin or characters.

1. _____

2. _____

3. _____

4. _____

5. _____

V. Audio Clip 4-4-5 includes three short listening passages. Each passage is followed by three true or false questions based on the content. After listening to each passage, decide whether each statement based on the content is true or false. Each passage will be read twice.

Passage 1

Notes: _____

_____

_____

a. 南京大学是一百多年以前成立的。　　　　　　T　　F

b. 南京大学是最早收女生的大学。　　　　　　　T　　F

c. 现在的南京大学有两千多学生。　　　　　　　T　　F

Passage 2

Notable words:

科举考试 (kējǔ kǎoshì, the Civil Service Exam)

祭拜 (jìbài, to worship)

孔子 (Kǒng Zǐ, Confucius)

Notes: _____

_____

_____

a. 夫子庙每年春节的时候都有灯会。	T	F
b. 以前参加科举考试的人，要到夫子庙来考。	T	F
c. 现在如果你去夫子庙，你可以在那儿逛街和参加考试。	T	F

Passage 3

明朝 (Míng cháo, the Ming Dynasty)

Notes: _____

_____

_____

a. 有名的北京烤鸭其实是明朝的时候从南京带来的。	T	F
b. 南京鸭和北京鸭不一样的地方是，南京鸭肥，北京鸭瘦。	T	F
c. 南京鸭是湖里的鸭子。北京鸭是河里的鸭子。	T	F

VI. In Audio Clip 4-4-6 you will hear some additional words that are introduced in the "Extend Your Knowledge" section of Lesson 4.4. After each word, you will be given 10 seconds to record your definition or explanation. You can take notes while listening. Record your answers on an audio recorder. If you do not have a recording device, you can write down your answers below in pinyin or Chinese characters.

Model:

You will hear	You will say
牙膏	刷牙用的白色的东西

You will hear	You will say
1.	
2.	
3.	
4.	
5.	
6.	
7.	
8.	

二 · 综合语言练习

I. **How do you say it in Chinese?**

1. Do you know where the Chinese speech contest will be held?

_____

2. A chartered bus will take us directly to the hotel.

_____

3. Please wear appropriate clothing in accordance with the weather conditions.

_____

4. Based on what you said, I'd better take my laptop with me.

_____

5. Your backpack is too small and can't fit so many books.

_____

6. According to our itinerary, we will arrive at the park around 3 p.m.

_____

7. Because the hotel has toiletries, you don't need to bring any.

_____

8. In order to protect the environment, it is best not to use disposable items.

_____

II. **Did David have the correct information?**

David wrote an email to Honghong's mother, asking to take a day off from his tutoring job. Compare David's email to the Lesson 4.4 Text. Did David get all the facts right? If not, write down the discrepancies (at least three) in the space below.

Send	Reply	Reply All	Forward	Print	Delete

红红妈妈：您好！

　　这个星期六我不能去您家辅导红红了。我们汉语班要去南京参加华东地区"大、中、小学生汉语演讲大赛"。我们星期六一大早去，早上七点左右到达南京。到了南京以后，先去吃早饭，然后就去南京大学参加比赛。

　　除了参加比赛以外，学校还组织了一些其他的活动。星期六晚上，我们要去参观南京的夫子庙。星期天上午我们去中山风景区。吃完午饭就回上海。

　　我不太清楚我们怎么去南京，一定是坐动车去吧。

　　下个星期三和星期六，我可以去辅导红红。星期三再见！

　　　　　　　　　　　　　　　　　　　　　　　大卫

课文说	大卫说

III. What things will Maria take to Nanjing?

Read the Lesson 4.4 Dialogue and list all the things that Maria will take to Nanjing.

IV. Match Them!

Match the phrases/sentences in columns A and B to make a logical sentence.

A	B
根据学生提出的建议，	1. 中国人在第二世纪初就发明了纸。
根据天气预报	2. 世界上的网民越来越多。
根据历史书说的，	3. 我们学校毕业生的高考成绩越来越好。
根据电视新闻，	4. 学校的图书馆星期六和星期天都开门。
根据医生的意见，	5. 明天要下大雪。
根据校长的报告，	6. 他在家休息了三天。

V. **Pair Activity: Our Itinerary**

Imagine that your class will take a trip to visit the West Coast of the United States. Because of a tight schedule, you will only be able to spend one day in San Francisco.

Step 1: Work in pairs. Based on the list of tourist attractions below, draft an itinerary that will capture the highlights of San Francisco.

旧金山旅游景点：	
渔 (yú) 人码头	Fisherman's Wharf
联合广场	Union Square
唐人街	Chinatown
金门大桥	Golden Gate Bridge
金门公园	Golden Gate Park
日本城	Japan Town
北滩 (tān)	North Beach
旧金山动物园	San Francisco Zoo
九曲 (qǔ) 花街	Lombard Crooked Street
艺术宫 (gōng)	The Exploratorium

我们的行程计划	
时间	活动

Step 2: Together with your partner, share your itinerary in class. (Be sure to keep your itinerary because you will need it for this lesson's written exercise.)

Step 3: After the presentation, work with your partner to create a tourist brochure for the town where you live. Your brochure must include the following information: what are the tourist attractions in your town? If someone is going to spend only one day in your town, what would you recommend this person see and visit? Create an itinerary using the form below.

"如果您来我们的城市玩一天" 行程建议	
时间	活动

VI. Pair Activity: A Packing List

Now it's time to pack for your trip. Everyone is allowed to take one small suitcase due to the limited space on the motor coach. You and your partner are tasked to draft a "packing list" for other students. Based on the information in the following chart, decide what should be included in the packing list.

我们的行程	洛杉矶 (Luòshānjī, Los Angeles)—旧金山—波特兰 (Bōtèlán, Portland) —西雅图 (Xīyǎtú, Seattle)
主要活动	参观旅游景点，参观博物馆，参观大学，听讲座
天气情况	下周美国加州的天气是晴天，气温在华氏 (Huáshì, Fahrenheit) 50度到72度。波特兰和西雅图的天气是有小雨，气温华氏45度到62度。
行李规定	每人可以带一个背包，和一个小箱子（最大：24″x13″x10″）

建议大家可以带以下的东西：	

VII. Class Debate: Which product is better for the environment?

Divide yourselves into two teams.

> **Team A:** You will argue for the pros of disposable products.
> **Team B:** You will argue for the cons of disposable products.

Step 1: Work as a team to talk about the pros or cons of disposable products.

Step 2: Hold a class debate.

汉语课：＿＿＿＿＿＿＿＿＿　　　学生姓名：＿＿＿＿＿＿＿＿＿

日　期：＿＿＿＿＿＿＿＿＿

三·写作练习

Based on the itinerary you and your partner created in Exercise V, write a short announcement (no more than 100 characters) to your class about your trip to San Francisco (or another city of your choice). You can refer to the Lesson 4.4 Text for the format of the announcement.

通知

_____

_____

_____

_____

_____

_____

_____

_____

_____

家长开放日
Open House Day for Parents

一·听力练习

 I. **Match Them!**

Match the words/phrases you hear in Audio Clip 4-5-1 with the definitions/explanations in Column B. Enter the corresponding numbers and words/phrases in Column A.

Column A 你听到的	Column B 意思
	这个词的意思是大家坐在一起讨论一个问题。
	这是在展览会上的一种工作。做这种工作的人告诉参观的人一个展览的内容和历史。
	这是爱好戏剧的学生组织的社团。
	这个词的意思是老师怎么教学生，用什么课本，怎么考试，什么的。
	这个词的意思是 一个人怎么想，对一件是有什么意见。
	这是喜欢唱歌的学生组织的社团。
	这个词的意思是学校定好一天请家长们来参观。
	这是每个老师都有的文件，上面写着每天在一门课上教什么，做什么活动。
	这是书法和中国画的展览。
	这是为了给要参加大学入学考试的学生和家长准备的文件。

II. Listen to the recording of the Lesson 4.5 Text first, and then answer the True/False questions in Audio Clip 4-5-2.

	1	2	3	4
对				
错				

III. Listen to the recording of the Lesson 4.5 Dialogue first, and then answer the True/False questions in Audio Clip 4-5-3.

	1	2	3	4
对				
错				

IV. Imagine that you are a student tour guide at your school's Open House, and you are having a conversation with a parent visitor. Listen carefully to the questions in Audio Clip 4-5-4 and record your answers on an audio recorder. You have 30 seconds to record your answers. If you do not have a recording device, you can write down your answers below in pinyin or characters.

1. _____

2. _____

3. _____

4. _____

5. _____

6. _____

V. Audio Clip 4-5-5 includes three short listening passages. Each passage is followed by three or four true or false questions based on the content. After listening to each passage, decide whether each statement based on the content is true or false. Each passage will be read twice.

<u>Passage 1</u>

Notes: _____

_____

_____

a. 大家要画蛇，因为他们要看看谁画画儿画得最好。　　T　　F

b. 汽水被大明喝了，因为他画得最快。　　T　　F

c. 画蛇添足这个成语告诉我们，不要做多余的没用的事　　T　　F

<u>Passage 2</u>

Notable words:

寺院 (sìyuàn, a Buddhist temple)　　　　生动 (vivid)

Notes: _____

_____

_____

a. 张僧繇 (Zhāng Sēngyóu) 画龙的时候没画眼睛，因为
他怕龙会飞走。　　T　　F

b. 张僧繇的朋友们都觉得画的龙能飞是不可能的。　　T　　F

c. 因为张僧繇给龙画上了眼睛，结果他画的四条龙最后
都飞到天上去了。　　T　　F

<u>Passage 3</u>

Notable words:

泥 (ní, mud, clay)　　　　清朝 (Qīng cháo, the Qing Dynasty)

巴拿马国际博览会 (Bānámǎ Guójì Bólǎnhuì, The Panama World Expo)

Notes: _____

_____

_____

a. 泥人开始的时候是给小孩子玩儿的。   T   F

b. 大家给张明山"泥人张"这个名字，因为他很会做泥人。 T   F

c. 泥人张的儿女们不愿意做泥人了，因为他们都上了大学。T   F

d. 如果你对做泥人有兴趣，你可以在中国美术学院上

     做泥人的课。   T   F

 VI. In Audio Clip 4-5-6 you will hear Chinese idioms and proverbs that have been previously introduced. After each idiom/proverb, you will be given 20 seconds to record your definition or explanation. You can take notes while listening. Record your answers on an audio recorder. If you do not have a recording device, you can write down your answers below in pinyin or Chinese characters.

Word Bank

画龙点睛	画蛇添足	欢天喜地	喜笑颜开	欢声笑语

Model:

You will hear	You will say
多子多福	这个成语的意思是儿子越多家里的生活就越好。

You will hear	You will say

二·综合语言练习

I. How do you say it in Chinese?

1. The school will hold "Parents' Day" (open house for parents) this Saturday.

_____

2. All of the classes will be open to parents.

_____

3. The principal will listen to parents' comments and suggestions.

_____

4. A teacher who teaches the senior class will give information on the college entrance exam.

_____

5. Students' artwork, essays, and science experiments are on display in the library.

_____

6. Students will have an open discussion with the teachers.

_____

7. Our class is in charge of the reception hosting the parents.

_____

8. Anyone can volunteer to be a guide for the art exhibition.

_____

II. **Parents' Day**

Based on the Lesson 4.5 Text, circle the activities that parents can attend on "Parents' Day."

参加学校运动会		吃午饭
跟老师座谈会	跟校长开座谈会	
参加招待会		
去体育馆看体育训练		去学生宿舍休息
去电脑房上网		跟学生一起吃点心

III. **What are they going to do for Parents' Day?**

Based on the Lesson 4.5 Dialogue, decide whether the following statements are true or false and circle the correct answer.

1. 汤姆上午要上课。		
2. 大卫上午要去参加座谈会。		
3. 玛丽娅要负责汉语班的座谈会。		
4. 凯丽要去弹钢琴。		
5. 大卫要去体育馆接待家长。		
6. 汤姆和明英要去看学生表演节目。		
7. 明英要负责展览的讲解工作。		
8. 汤姆要去电脑房接待家长。		
9. 玛丽娅要准备科学实验展览。		
10. 凯丽要当讲解员。		

IV. Mixer Bingo: What should be required?

Your school is launching a "Year of World Languages and Cultures." A questionnaire has been designed to get students' input.

Step 1: Complete the questionnaire for yourself.

问题	同意/不同意，为什么？
所有的老师都应该会说外语。	
所有的课都应该用外语上。	
所有的学生都应该去国外旅游。	
所有的学生都应该上外语课。	
所有的学生都应该念国际新闻。	
所有的学生都应该学习世界地理。	
所有的学生都应该参加国际文化日的活动。	
所有的学生都应该学习世界历史。	
所有的学生都应该听外国文化讲座。	
所有的学生都应该看一些外国电影。	
所有的学生都应该听一些外国音乐。	
所有的学生都应该参观关于外国的艺术展览。	

Step 2: Choose nine proposals from the list above to fill your bingo grid.

Step 3: Walk around the classroom and interview your classmates. You can only ask one question at a time. The student who gets three positive answers in a row (horizontal, vertical, or diagonal) wins the game. When it is your turn to answer a question, make sure you answer according to what you have written down in the questionnaire.

Model:　　问题：你同意所有的学生都应该会说外语吗？

　　　　　　回答：我同意，因为……。(Or 我不同意，因为……。)

V. Pair Activity: Mini-Dialogue

Suppose you are parents who have attended the "Parents' Day" activities.

A: **You start**	B: **Your partner starts**
• Tell B your son attends the high school. Ask if B has children attending this school. • Tell B your son is doing so-so. According to your son, some classes are not very interesting. Ask if B's daughter is doing well. • Ask if B will talk to the English teacher today. • Tell B it is a good idea. You will go to an open discussion hosted by the principal.	• Tell A your daughter attends the school. Ask if A's son is doing well in school. • Tell A your daughter is doing well in math, chemistry, and physical education, but not very well in English. Your daughter doesn't like the English class. • Tell A you are going to look at the English teacher's lesson plans and attend an open discussion with the teachers.

A: **Your partner starts**	B: **You start**
• Tell B you were very busy. You observed three classes, went to two open discussions, and listened to three reports made by teachers. Ask what B did.	• Ask if A had a good time during Parents' Day.
• Ask if B saw the English teacher's lesson plans.	• Tell A you observed a class, attended an open discussion, talked to the principal, and saw the exhibition of teachers' lesson plans.
• Ask if B has met the English teacher.	• Tell A you didn't, but you saw a research paper written by the English teacher.
• Tell B it's best to talk to his or her daughter and find out why she doesn't like the English class.	• Tell A you did. The English teacher was playing piano at the school's performance. She is quite young and looks like a very nice lady.
	• Agree with A.

VI. A Parent's Blog

After attending "Parents' Day," a parent wrote the following blog post to describe his experience.

Step 1: Read the blog posting and answer the questions following it.

上个星期五，我去上海国际学校参加了"家长开放日"的活动。我儿子在国际学校上高二，他挺聪明的，可是学习成绩马马虎虎。眼看明年他就要参加高考了，我和他妈妈都非常担心，怕他考不上一个好大学。这次我去参加家长日活动，就是想去看看国际学校的教学情况。

学校为家长安排了很多活动，有些是关于教学的，比如听课、听校长报告、跟学生开座谈会。还有一些展览，可以让我们看到学校的教学成绩。另外有些活动是为了让家长了解学校，比方说，我们可以参观学校的图书馆、电脑房、学生宿舍什么的。

上海国际学校我去过很多次了，所以我这次去，主要是去听课。我听了三堂课：数学、历史和汉语。数学课上得不错，老师讲题讲得很清楚，学生也有许多做题的机会。历史课的老师讲得很多。她讲课的时候，学生都在下面记笔记。汉语课那天是汉语口试。老师把学生一个一个叫进教室来，每个学生都要先听录音，再把录音里的故事告诉老师。如果他们的故事说得不清楚，老师就会问问题。我觉得录音挺长的，汉语考试真不容易。听了课以后，我觉得国际学校的教学还不错。

参加了家长开放日以后，我更觉得，儿子学习成绩不够好主要还是他自己的问题。他不怎么爱学习，做作业总是三心二意。我怎么才能让他一心一意地学习呢？很希望听到大家的意见。如果您有教育孩子的好主意，请告诉我。谢谢！

1. 这位家长为什么决定去参加家长开放日的活动？

_____

2. 家长开放日有哪些关于教学的活动？

_____

3. 这位家长去听了什么课？

_____

4. 听课的时候，这位家长看到了什么？

_____

_____

5. 这位家长想得到什么帮助？

_____

Step 2: Write a 50-character response to this blog posting.

_____

_____

_____

_____

_____

_____

VII. Class Project: Welcome to My School!

Task: You will create a Chinese brochure for your school. In your brochure make sure to include the following information:

1. The name, address, phone number, and website of your school.
2. Type of school (public or private, single-sex or co-ed?)
3. Basic school facilities
4. Basic course offerings and graduation requirements
5. Basic student service resources

Evaluation:

You will be evaluated based on:

1. Task completion
2. Incorporation of a variety of vocabulary and sentence structures
3. Artistic creativity

汉语课：＿＿＿＿＿＿＿＿＿　　　学生姓名：＿＿＿＿＿＿＿＿＿

日期：　　＿＿＿＿＿＿＿＿＿

三·写作练习

Choose one of the questions below, and write a short essay (no more than 300 characters) in Chinese.

1. 如果你们学校要举办家长开放日，你觉得家长开放日应该有什么活动？

2. 你希望你的家长来参加家长开放日吗？为什么？

3. 如果家长和老师有比较多的联系，会不会帮助一个学生的学习？为什么？

4. 你觉得如果一个学生学习成绩不好，谁应该负比较多的责任？为什么？

4.6 第四单元复习
Review of Unit 4

一·口头报告

Choose one of the topics from the list below to give an oral presentation in class. Your presentation must meet the following criteria:

1. It must discuss a specific person or a concrete thing, as the topics for the presentations are very broad.
2. It must have a beginning, a middle, and an end.
3. It must include as much detail as possible.
4. It must last no longer than two minutes.

After you have chosen the topic, please write an outline for your presentation. You can write the outline on a separate sheet of paper. If your teacher allows, you can also transfer the outline to an index card as a reminder when you give the presentation.

Topic 1. 我最喜欢的运动员

Topic 2. 我们国家的节日食品

Topic 3. 我们这里最好的地方

Topic 4. 一件出门旅行必须要带的东西

Topic 5. 欢迎你来我们学校参观！

Topic 6. 我最喜欢的中国菜

Topic 7. 我最喜欢的成语故事

Topic 8. 我最喜欢的中国艺术

二·综合语言练习

I. True or False

Based on the Lesson 4.6 Text, decide whether the following statements are true or false.

	对	错
1. 老师、学生和家长参加了国际文化日的活动。		
2. 国际学校有来自三十多个国家和地区的学生和老师。		
3. 国际学校有三十多个外语班。		
4. 外语班的学生介绍了他们学习的语言和文化。		
5. 英语班的学生介绍了美国、英国、澳大利亚、新西兰的情况。		
6. 汉语班的活动最受大家的欢迎。		
7. 汉语班介绍了中国各地的农业出产对饮食的影响。		
8. 汉语班的同学被分成四个小组，做了四个地方的菜。		
9. 观众都觉得山东组做的饺子是最好吃的。		
10. 国际文化日让大家有机会了解各国文化。		

II. What is the procedure to register for the online math contest?

Based on the Lesson 4.6 Dialogue, rearrange the scrambled sentences below into a logical paragraph that describes the math contest.

1. 教育网站根据学生的年龄把他们分到不同的竞赛组。
2. 这个数学竞赛主要比赛口算的能力。
3. 小学组和中学组做的是不同的数学题。
4. 我来介绍一下"国际网上数学竞赛"。
5. 哪个学生算得又快又好，就可以多得分。
6. 参加这个数学竞赛是免费的。
7. 要参加数学竞赛，可以先上网报名。
8. 网站让两个或更多的学生一起在网上比赛。

List the statements in a logical order: _____

III. Group Project: School Activities

Since we have learned expressions used to discuss school activities in Unit 4, let's host an activity design contest.

Step 1: Form groups of three or four students. Brainstorm two activities that your group would like to organize, decide who will be in charge of creating certain documents for the activities, and write the results in the form below. The documents that you need to prepare are:

1. An advertisement
2. Registration requirements and procedures
3. Logistics: the location and rules of the contest, venues for a celebration, etc.

活动	文件	由谁负责
1.	广告	
	报名表和要求	
	活动规定、条件、地点、费用等	
2.	广告	
	报名表和要求	
	活动规定、条件、地点、费用等	

Step 2: Begin to draft or create each document according to your assignments.

Step 3: Participate in the contest: Display your documents in class and explain your activity, procedures, and rules to your classmates. The group that comes up with the most interesting activity wins the contest.

IV. Pair Activity: Who said what?

Step 1: Work in pairs. Take turns to read the accounts on your worksheet. While your partner speaks, you should listen carefully and match what you hear with one of the pictures below. Note: There are more pictures than self accounts.

A's sheet

1	我们汉语班的同学在国际文化日要举行烹调表演。我们打算给大家介绍广东的点心。做广东点心不容易，需要很多准备工作。我的工作是准备厨房用具。为了买到蒸笼，我去了很多商店，最后在一个中国超市里买到了。
3	大卫参加了学校运动会的体操比赛。虽然他的比赛成绩不够理想，但是我们班的同学都觉得他是一个很好的体操运动员。
5	上个星期我们班去一个动物园参观，看到了大熊猫。我们还跟动物园的经理座谈，了解到这只大熊猫是中国政府借给我国的。过了十年以后，大熊猫要回到中国去。

B's sheet

2	昨天我们坐车去校外考察。在路上，车坏了。司机打电话让学区给我们另外一辆车。可是因为交通很堵，我们等了一个多小时，那辆车才来。
4	我们开晚会要做中国饭。做中国饭就需要炒菜。学生餐厅里没有炒菜锅。我想中国人家里一定有炒菜锅，所以就问了丁老师。她就把她家的炒菜锅借给我们了。
6	我妹妹在东方中学上学。上个星期，东方中学举办了家长开放日。那天，东方中学的学生在大礼堂表演了节目。你看，那个弹吉他的女孩子就是我妹妹。

Step 2: Compare notes with your partner. See if you agree on the matches.

V. Board Game: Guess That Word

Work in pairs. Take turns to guess the word based on the definition given. If one partner can't guess the word, the other has a chance to make a guess. At the end of the game, see who has guessed more words correctly.

词的意思	A	B
去看老师怎么上课		
可以在那个地方举行田径比赛		
住在一个地方的人		
让大家晚上去买东西的地方		
很早以前造的房子		
停船的地方		
做烤肉需要用的		

很多人同时说话		
忘了这个，忘了那个		
让大家看怎么做饭		
每天的旅行计划		
把很多作品放在一起让别人参观		
老师上课的计划		
运动需要用的东西		

VI. Online Chat Room

You are in an online chat room. Type your questions and answers in Chinese.

网友一： 这个周末我和朋友要去上海旅游。上海有哪些有名的旅游景点？

网友二： 我也没去过上海。听说那里有许多商店，可以去那里买东西。

你： _____

网友一： 哦，你是说，外滩是最有名的景点之一吗？外滩有什么特别的？我看到过外滩的照片。有许多欧洲式的建筑。你知道那些建筑是什么时候造的吗？

你： _____

网友二： 我在英文网站上看到，外国人把外滩叫作 "the Bund"。你知道这是为什么吗？

你： _____

网友一： 听说外滩有一个有名的公园。是什么公园啊？

你： _____

网友二：　除了外滩以外，上海还有什么可以去参观的地方？有没有博物馆？

你：　　　_____

网友一：　你说在上海应该玩几天？

你：　　　_____

网友一：　谢谢你的建议。

CREDITS

Murray Thomas contributed the drawings on the following pages:

8, 58, 133

Qiguang Xu contributed the drawing on the following page:

8

Landong Xu contributed the drawings on the following pages:

48, 58, 105, 133

Augustine Liu contributed the drawing on the following page:

92

洋洋兔动漫

133